SHIPS IN FOCUS
Ellerman Lines

John Clarkson

Roy Fenton

CITY OF CANBERRA *1927; see page 35.*

Published 1993 by John and Marion Clarkson
18 Franklands, Longton, Preston, PR4 5PD United Kingdom.

© 1993 John Clarkson and Roy Fenton

Typeset by Highlight Type Bureau Limited, Shipley.
Printed by Amadeus Press Limited, Huddersfield.
Bound and finished by Woods (Bradford) Ltd.

ISBN 0 9521179 0 8

D0417447

FOREWORD

It was back in 1956 that I first became interested in collecting photographs of ships. The first six I bought, which I still have, were bought from Basil Feilden of Birkdale for the princely sum of 3/-: 6d each. From that day on I admired his work and, when I first attempted printing in 1963, tried to match it, but with little success. Over the years I have gathered together various collections of negatives, but you can imagine my feelings when in 1983 I was fortunate enough to buy the bulk of Basil's negatives, The Feilden Collection.

Basil was born in Yorkshire in 1908, one of the sons of a manufacturer's agent. By the twenties the family had moved to Merseyside and Basil started photographing ships and selling the resulting prints through shops in Liverpool and Birkenhead. His first camera was a Box Brownie, but he soon progressed to an Ensign DeLuxe reflex which used half plate sheet film or glass plates. Travelling about on a New Imperial 350cc motorcycle with the camera strapped on the back, Basil took photographs on both sides of the Mersey. He made one visit to Southampton and a couple to Barrow to photograph particular liners, and three to the Clyde for the launches of the QUEEN MARY and QUEEN ELIZABETH, and for the sailing of the former. He was assisted at times by his brother Alan who later became a photographer with Stewart Bales at Liverpool, but printing stopped when materials became unavailable in 1939. Basil joined the RAF, but in May 1940 he bought the remaining negatives of another well-known photographer, Cooper of Egremont. These still form an important part of the collection.

Basil started taking photographs again about 1950, but seems to have finished in the late fifties although he continued to print until the late sixties. The collection then remained unused until 1983. Basil still lives in Birkdale, and it is only in recent months that his motorcycle, put away in an outhouse for many years, was scrapped after it fell to pieces when being moved.

Other photographs included in this book have been taken by Harry Stewart of Preston, John McRoberts of Wallasey, Des Harris of Penarth and Peter Foxley of Malaysia - unfortunately all no longer with us - photographers in Australia and South Africa unknown to me, Paul Boot of Barnston, Tom Rayner on the Isle of Wight and myself. Should I have missed anyone, I hope they will forgive me.

My grateful thanks go to Roy Fenton for writing the introduction and the captions. Without Roy, I doubt if the book would ever have become more than an idea in my head. Thank you also to Richard Cook and his staff at Amadeus Press for their assistance and advice. Last but not least, I am grateful to Marion and my family for their encouragement and support.

As Thomas Hardy, poet and novelist, wrote "The petty done, the undone vast! The more written the more seems to remain to be written, and the night cometh." I hope that you will enjoy this book: if it is a success, then more will follow. I now hand over to Roy for a brief history of the Ellerman group before we proceed to the photographs.

John Clarkson, Longton, May 1993.

CITY OF MANCHESTER
Barclay, Curle and Co. Ltd., Glasgow; 1902, 5551gt.
This classic Mersey view shows City Lines' CITY OF MANCHESTER. Her career seems to have been relatively uneventful, and after thirty years on City Line and later Ellerman and Bucknall services, she was sold to Italian breakers and demolished at La Spezia in 1933.

THE ELLERMAN ACHIEVEMENT

John Reeves Ellerman was one of the most successful of British shipping financiers. The empire he built may not have been as large as that of Kylsant's Royal Mail Group, but it was far more durable. He owned fewer ships than his erstwhile partner Christopher Furness, but his family's control was maintained far longer, and his ships were operated as a much more homogeneous fleet. As the photographs in this book will show, Ellerman ships were amongst the most readily recognisable in the British merchant marine.

The thirty-year old Ellerman had already achieved some success as a financier when, in 1892, he joined with Christopher Furness to float a company to purchase the fleet of Frederick Leyland. Although well established in the Mediterranean and North Atlantic trades, the Leyland Line had many obsolete ships, but under Ellerman's management the company flourished, expanded its trades, paid good dividends and even absorbed the twenty ships of the West India and Pacific Steamship Co. Ltd. Having established a successful concern, in 1901 the partners negotiated the sale of the Leyland business to J. Pierpoint Morgan's International Mercantile Marine at a substantial profit, enhancing even further Ellerman's reputation. He remained as chairman of Leyland, but agreed not to compete with the company in the main North Atlantic trades. Instead he looked east.

Ellerman retained twenty of the Leyland ships and an interest in the Mediterranean and some other trades, and to these quickly added the business of Papayanni and Company of Liverpool. This family concern was typical of those which Ellerman was to acquire: well-established but in need of capital to modernise its fleet of eight ships. To own the twenty ex-Leyland ships, Ellerman established the London, Liverpool and Ocean Shipping Co. Ltd. In spite of a grandiose title, its trade was mainly to the Mediterranean, but Ellerman had his sights set wider. At the company's first general meeting he announced that the City Line of Glasgow had been acquired, and that he was negotiating to buy the Hall Line of Liverpool. Both were respected family concerns trading mainly to India.

Ellerman had bought the Papayanni ships and half the shares in City and Hall Lines in his own right, but early in 1902 he sold these to the London, Liverpool and Ocean Shipping Co. Ltd., which was reformed as Ellerman Lines Ltd. Within months was added the small fleet of Westcott and Laurance, trading between London and the Mediterranean.

In the next few years Ellerman Lines Ltd. expanded its routes carefully, partly by joint services like that with Allan Line to the River Plate. In 1908, however, came another major acquisition, Bucknall Steamship Lines Ltd. The company was experiencing financial difficulties due partly to a decline in its South African trade following the end of the Boer War. Such was Ellerman's standing that he was invited by the Bucknall board to make a bid for the company. Unlike previous acquisitions which painted up Ellerman's orange, white and black funnel, Bucknall ships retained their distinctive funnel colours for a quarter of a century.

Expansion continued up to and through the First World War, with routes established to East Africa, the Persian Gulf, the Far East, Australasia and North America. In 1916 came one of Ellerman's greatest coups: his personal acquisition of Thomas Wilson, Sons and Co. Ltd. of Hull, reputedly the largest private shipping company in the world. Although quickly renamed Ellerman's Wilson Line Ltd., its operations were kept largely separate from those of Ellerman Lines Ltd., and only a few ships transferred to the parent company appear in this book. Another wartime acquisition was a part interest in shipbuilder William Gray and Co. Ltd. This move helped the group replace its many war losses, along with heavy purchases of ex-German tonnage.

The long depression in trade between the wars meant that this period was not one of great expansion. The only important acquisition was Montgomerie and Workman Ltd., the London agents of City Line, in 1920. The company's name was to appear as owners of several ships during the next sixteen years.

John Reeves Ellerman died in July 1933, leaving a personal fortune of some £40 million. His was a hard, if not impossible, act to follow. His only son, who shared his name, was a philanthropic, scholarly man with a passion for anonymity. With Ellerman the days of the great British shipping entrepreneurs had passed, and although the group prospered for almost another fifty years, its great days of expansion were over.

Losses during the Second World War were, if anything, worse than in the First, with Ellerman cargo and passenger liners proving their value as transports and troop carriers. The price in terms of men and ships was high, as all too many of the captions in this book tell.

Post-war rebuilding was tackled with energy, and the Ellerman fleet remained a major force in liner shipping. But independence for India and Pakistan, the emergence of new maritime nations and the shipping revolution brought about by container ships, bulk carriers and other specialised vessels helped to push Britain from her position of eminence, and with her fell many of her shipping empires. There was one post-war purchase; in 1958 the group bought the small Mossgiel Steamship Co. Ltd. which operated a service from Glasgow to the Mediterranean.

The first deliveries of pure container ships at the end of the sixties heralded a massive decline in the size of the fleet. Ellerman took shares in Associated Container Transportation Ltd. and Ben Line Containers Ltd., whilst their Mediterranean services were operated initially by chartered container ships. When the second John Reeves Ellerman died in 1973, the fleet consisted of less than forty ships compared with over one hundred in its prime. Fleet decline was eventually accompanied by heavy financial losses and in 1983 the group was sold. There was later a short-lived management buy-back, but in 1987 the Trafalgar House group purchased Ellerman's shipping interests and merged them with its Cunard activities as Cunard-Ellerman. Today, with Ellerman flags and funnel gone, only the occasional and usually chartered container vessel with a City name is a reminder of one of the Britain's greatest fleets.

About the captions

In arranging the photographs we have departed from a strict chronological sequence in order to group related ships together. In this way we hope to show how the design of Ellerman ships evolved over the group's eighty years of shipowning. The captions focus on interesting features of the ship and her history, and give builder, date, gross tonnage when acquired and fate. Ownership of Ellerman ships was a complex matter, and to avoid too much detail we have merely indicated for which of the four main shipping lines the ship was intended. Transfers from one line's service to another were very common: changes of ownership less so. Neither have we given full details of machinery builders. The reader can assume that, unless otherwise stated, all ships built before 1950 have steam reciprocating engines, and that those after that date are motorships.

Acknowledgements

Duncan Haw's *Merchant Fleets 16: Ellerman Lines* has proved invaluable in helping allocate ships to classes and owners, and has given guidance on the ships' careers. The latter have been checked from the usual sources: *Lloyds Register, Lloyds Confidential Index, Lloyds War Loss Books, Marine News* and *Sea Breezes*. James Taylor's eulogy *Ellermans: A Wealth of Shipping* has also been consulted. The authors would also like to thank the World Ship Society's Central Record and the Shipping Information Services of Lloyds Register of Shipping for help and facilities. In contrast to the rest of the Ellerman group, Wilson Line has been poorly served by historians and the World Ship Society's forthcoming history and fleet list by John Harrower is commended to readers.

Roy Fenton, Wimbledon, May 1993

FLAMINIAN

Earle's Shipbuilding and Engineering Co. Ltd., Hull; 1914, 3439gt.
The only photograph in this book taken before the First World War shows the FLAMINIAN on her trials in the Humber. Within a year she was sunk, caught by the German submarine U-28 on 29th March 1915 south west of the Scilly Isles whilst on a voyage from the Clyde to South Africa.

EARLY HALL LINE STEAMERS

CREWE HALL
Palmer's Shipbuilding and Iron Co. Ltd., Jarrow; 1898, 4218gt

Getting underway CREWE HALL leaves little doubt that she is a coal burner. She was built for the Sun Shipping Co. Ltd., but when the company was re-organised prior to its sale in 1899 her ownership was transferred to the Hall Line Ltd. The title Hall Line had been used informally for some thirty years by managers Robert Alexander and Co. Under Ellerman ownership CREWE HALL was to serve out her natural life of thirty years, being broken at Newport in 1929.

WALTON HALL
Barclay, Curle and Co. Ltd, Glasgow; 1907, 4932gt

The Mersey boatmen seem more interested in the camera than the rope lowered from the fo'c'sle of the WALTON HALL. She appears to have had an almost blameless, if rather dull, life and was broken up in 1931 on the river on which she was born.

EARLY HALL LINE STEAMERS (cont)

STANLEY HALL
Palmer's Shipbuilding and Iron Co. Ltd., Jarrow; 1894, 4104gt.

When this photograph of her was taken in a blustery Mersey the STANLEY HALL was reaching the end of a long career. She was broken up at Rosyth in 1928.

CITY OF MADRAS
Palmer's Shipbuilding and Iron Co. Ltd., Jarrow; 1903, 4684gt

Originally intended to be the RUFFORD HALL, the CITY OF MADRAS was delivered just after the acquisition of Hall Line by Ellerman. A policy of giving all ships City names was not relentlessly pursued, however, and several later vessels were delivered with Hall names, including a further RUFFORD HALL. CITY OF MADRAS was sold to Italian shipbreakers in 1931.

NEWBY HALL
Barclay, Curle and Co. Ltd., Glasgow; 1905, 4388gt.

Between 1903 and 1906 Hall Line took delivery of eight basically similar steamers, distinguished by a wide steam pipe which was painted to match the funnel. Of the four which survived the First World War, three went to Greek owners: NEWBY HALL becoming the YIANNIS of Andros in 1930. In 1936 she was sold to France, and as AMIRAL PIERRE was scuttled in the Mozambique Channel on 30th September 1942 to avoid capture by the Royal Navy.

CITY OF BOMBAY
Palmer's Shipbuilding and Iron Co. Ltd, Jarrow; 1910, 5186gt

CITY OF BOMBAY was one of a group of four ships which introduced a new profile to the Ellerman fleet, with a hatch at the after end of the bridge deck served by a pair of king posts. After a modest 22 years' service CITY OF BOMBAY was broken up on the Clyde in 1932.

The large piece of steelwork just forward of her bridge is intriguing: close examination of the original print suggests it is not an unwieldy item of deck cargo, but a coal hoist under tow on the Mersey.

CITY OF DUNKIRK
Barclay, Curle and Co. Ltd., Glasgow; 1912, 5861gt.

Between CITY OF BOMBAY and CITY OF DUNKIRK the long poop deck carrying a hatch had made its appearance: it was to be an enduring feature of the Ellerman fleet. CITY OF DUNKIRK gave excellent service, passing virtually unscathed through both world wars. In 1950 she was sold to Italy, and as the MARILEN and later MINERVA traded for her Genoese owners until broken up at La Spezia in 1959.

CITY OF CALCUTTA
Workman, Clark and Co. Ltd., Belfast; 1903, 7492gt, 179 passengers.

George Smith, founder of City Line, married a Margaret Workman whose family went on to become shipbuilders at Belfast. City Line ordered many ships from their yard, and the association long survived the line's sale to Ellerman: CITY OF CALCUTTA being the first of many passenger ships which the group had built there.

As a wartime transport for the Indian Expeditionary Force CITY OF CALCUTTA escaped hostile action, but had one violent encounter when she collided with the BURUTU in St. George's Channel during the dark, squally night of 3rd October 1918. The Elder, Dempster steamer sank with heavy loss of life.

CITY OF CALCUTTA herself survived, and after a period in lay up was sold to Japanese breakers in 1935, making the voyage east under the name CALCUT: changing a ship's name by obliterating a few letters not being purely a post-war phenomenon.

CITY OF YORK
Workman, Clark and Co. Ltd., Belfast; 1903, 7705gt, 165 passengers.

CITY OF YORK was a slightly bigger and more powerful version of CITY OF CALCUTTA. Surviving the war, like her near sister she took some of the American and Indian Line sailings from New York during the twenties. Retired in 1936, she was renamed CITY and taken to Japan for breaking up.

In this photograph she is clearly preparing to sail from the Mersey: the position of her boats suggesting that lifeboat practice is underway.

CITY OF LONDON
Workman, Clark and Co. Ltd., Belfast; 1907, 8896gt, 336 passengers.

As City Line's Liverpool to Bombay passenger trade grew in the first years of Ellerman ownership larger ships with greater passenger accommodation were required. These culminated in the CITY OF LONDON: it was to be another three decades before the group built a larger and faster ship.

In 1916 CITY OF LONDON was converted to an Armed Merchant Cruiser and used to patrol the South China Sea, although she failed to catch any German raiders. Reconditioned by her builders in 1919 she returned to City Line routes, but in the early thirties she was used on the Ellerman and Bucknall passenger service to South and East Africa, painting up the appropriate funnel colours. This photograph was taken between 1935 and 1939, when she had returned to City Line's Indian service and had finally acquired a grey hull, which certainly suited the old lady.

During her second war she was called up early. As a troop transport her finest hour probably came during April 1941 when she evacuated 3,700 troops from Crete to Alexandria. Her war service left her worn out, however. With age against her she was not considered worthy of reconditioning, and was broken up at Dalmuir in 1946.

CITY OF POONA
Swan, Hunter and Wigham Richardson Ltd., Wallsend; 1912, 7467gt, 138 passengers.

This fine photograph proves that City Line vessels looked smart even with black hulls. CITY OF POONA had a relatively peaceful career, but was a victim of the slump in world trade, being broken up in Japan in 1934 at the comparatively early age of 22 years. She made her final voyage east simply named POONA.

CITY OF KARACHI

Workman, Clark and Co. Ltd., Belfast; 1905, 5547gt, 94 passengers.

The CITY OF KARACHI is seen here in May 1934, laid up and awaiting a fate which was only months away. In October she was sold for scrapping, and as the KARACHI made her way to Japan.

Although officially a City Line ship, she finished her days wearing "Bucknall's teeth" on her funnel, a relic of the periods she spent running on Ellerman and Bucknall services.

MATOPPO

William Hamilton and Co. Ltd., Port Glasgow; 1905, 5280gt.

The MATOPPO of 1905 is also seen right at the end of her career, at the Preston shipbreaking yard of T.W. Ward Ltd., where she arrived late in 1930.

Built for Bucknall Steamship Lines Ltd., she was the first of the fleet transferred to other Ellerman routes, although a formal transfer to the Ellerman and Bucknall Steamship Co. Ltd. had to wait until 1914. Ellerman funnel colours came much later: probably during her very last years.

CITY OF SWANSEA
Armstrong, Whitworth and Co. Ltd., Newcastle; 1907, 4641gt.

CITY OF SWANSEA had been built for the independent Bucknall Steamship Lines Ltd. as KATUNA, a name she kept until 1929. In 1937 she was sold to the predecessors of the South American Saint Line Ltd. and renamed ST. GLEN. Her subsequent career was brief, however, as she was bombed and strafed by German aircraft off Aberdeen on 6th September 1940. Bound for Hull from South America at the time, she sank with the loss of three lives.

CITY OF WINNIPEG
Workman, Clark and Co. Ltd., Belfast; 1910, 6113gt.

As KANSAS, this was the first ship completed for the Bucknall Steamship Lines Ltd. after Ellerman acquired the company. Renaming CITY OF WINNIPEG had to wait until 1926, and when this photograph was taken in September 1930 she had not acquired the Ellerman funnel. At the end of 1934 she was sold to Japanese breakers, and sailed from Houston to Kobe officially known simply as WINNY.

MALATIAN
Earle's Shipbuilding and Engineering Co. Ltd., Hull; 1914, 3437gt.

The well-loaded MALATIAN has a very purposeful look in this June 1934 shot, accentuated by her well-raked counter stern. In the twenties she strayed far from her normal Mediterranean haunts, and operated a feeder service for Ellerman and Bucknall between Australia and the Dutch East Indies.

Sold to Italy in 1937 as SANTA MARIA, she was taken over by Germany when Italy surrendered, but paid the price when sunk by Allied aircraft at Venice in October 1944.

ROUMELIAN
Palmer's Shipbuilding and Iron Co. Ltd., Jarrow; 1914, 2687gt.

For ships intended for the Mediterranean services a naming scheme was used which Ellerman had inherited with his interest in the Leyland Line. ROUMELIAN took her inspiration from the ROUMELIA, built in 1877 for the Papayanni family and which long outlasted the province of the Ottoman Empire after which she was named.

Like MALATIAN she was sold to Italy, becoming DREPANUM in 1937. She too was lost after being taken over by Germany, being sunk in collision with the steamer LIPPE (see page 21) in the Baltic on 20th November 1943.

HALL LINE PASSENGER SHIPS

CITY OF MARSEILLES

Palmer's Shipbuilding and Iron Co. Ltd., Jarrow; 1913, 8250gt, 195 passengers.

CITY OF MARSEILLES was the largest of Hall Line's small quota of passenger ships, but in this September 1937 photograph her size is disguised somewhat as her white paint has not been carried down to main deck level.

She had a long and adventurous career. She was shot at by a U-boat in November 1915, and in 1916 rescued survivors from P. & O.'s torpedoed ARABIA. In the twenties she ran out of New York, and also did some trooping to India. In the Second World War she survived mine damage in January 1940 only to break her back after stranding off Ceylon in January 1943. She was on a voyage from Liverpool to Calcutta.

CITY OF CAIRO

Earle's Shipbuilding and Engineering Co. Ltd., Hull; 1915, 7672gt, 176 passengers.

Hall Line's CITY OF CAIRO began her life in one war, and ended it in another as one of the group's most tragic losses.

On 6th November 1942 she was crossing the South Atlantic on a typical wartime passage home from Bombay via Table Bay and Pernambuco, when torpedoed by U-68. Her complement was 296, including 100 passengers, but accounts differ as to how many were lost. What is not in doubt is the sufferings of the survivors: including weeks spent in open boats, eventual rescue by a German blockade runner which was then scuttled, a further lifeboat voyage, rescue by a U-boat which was depth charged, followed by internment in a prisoner-of-war camp.

CITY OF NORWICH

William Gray and Co. Ltd., West Hartlepool; 1913, 6382gt.

As if by decree, 1913 saw cruiser sterns introduced to all the Ellerman companies: CITY OF NORWICH having the first in Hall Line's fleet.

CITY OF NORWICH came through the First World War unscathed, and also escaped the large scale scrappings of the thirties. Her survival through a further war meant that she achieved over forty years in the fleet, and was not sold until the post-war rebuilding programme was well underway. Even then she could still find employment, and as the Italian-owned MARINUCCI she sailed under the Panama flag for four years until broken up at Yokohama in 1959.

CITY OF SHANGHAI

Earle's Shipbuilding and Engineering Co. Ltd., Hull; 1917, 5828gt.

Although Ellerman later bought a number of war standard and ex-German ships which had long bridge decks, Hall Line's CITY OF SHANGHAI was unique in being built for the group with this layout.

She was lost during a remarkably round about voyage. Wartime routing took her from the Tyne to Turkey via the West Indies, from where she would have made her way across the South Atlantic, round the Cape and through the Suez Canal. But en route to Table Bay on 11th May 1941 she was torpedoed by U-103 and sank with the loss of eight lives.

CITY OF BIRMINGHAM
William Gray and Co. Ltd., West Hartlepool, 1917, 6182gt.

City Line's CITY OF BIRMINGHAM was a miniature version of contemporary Hall Line ships being built at West Hartlepool. At a time when shipyards were desperately trying to replace losses that were threatening to cripple Great Britain, would it not have made better sense to build more ships to the same design?

Some doubtful logic also led to her loss in the subsequent conflict. Having safely reached Scotland from Beira with a valuable general cargo she was promptly routed to Hull, which thanks to German aircraft, E-boats and mines must have been one of the least safe of British ports. Shortly after leaving her coastal convoy off Spurn Point on 16th August 1940 she hit a mine and sank, although fortunately without loss of life.

CITY OF FLORENCE
William Gray and Co. Ltd., West Hartlepool; 1918, 6862gt.

During her 38 years with Hall Line CITY OF FLORENCE must have visited the Mersey many times, as in this photograph. At the end of her last voyage to Liverpool in 1956 she could still find a buyer, a London Greek investing £285,000 in her. MOUNT OLYMPUS was a fitting new name for a venerable and imposing lady, and as this she sailed under the Liberian flag until 1959 when she was broken up in Japan.

15

CITY OF NEWCASTLE
William Gray and Co. Ltd., West Hartlepool; 1915, 6921gt.

A large number of Ellerman ships met violent ends during the First World War, but Hall Line's CITY OF NEWCASTLE had a violent beginning to her life. Whilst fitting out at West Hartlepool on 16th December 1914 she was damaged by shells from the German battleships which bombarded several coastal towns.

After this baptism of fire she managed to survive both world wars, although in July 1943 she was damaged by an aerial torpedo during the Sicilian invasion. Sold in May 1951 she became the MARINUCCI for the same Italian owners who later bought the CITY OF NORWICH. A little over a year later, and now under the Panama flag, she arrived at La Spezia for demolition.

CITY OF HANKOW
William Gray and Co. Ltd., West Hartlepool; 1915, 7369gt.

Like her near sister CITY OF NEWCASTLE, CITY OF HANKOW was registered under the ownership of the City of Oran Steamship Co. Ltd., with Hall Line as managers.

The fate of CITY OF HANKOW is a reminder that the normal hazards of the sea are undiminished by war. On 18th December 1942 she was wrecked on South Point just to the north of Saldanha Bay, South Africa. This was her first port of call during a voyage from Liverpool to Durban and Beira with general cargo.

CITY OF BRISBANE
Swan, Hunter and Wigham Richardson Ltd., Wallsend; 1920, 7138gt.

Such was the scale of losses to U-boats during 1917 and 1918 that even Ellerman's energetic building programme could not keep pace. Of eight cargo liners built to the same design for Hall Line and delivered from 1917, two were lost in this way, including the first CITY OF BRISBANE.

On 2nd August 1940 the second of the name, seen here, was also to become a war loss, bombed and set on fire by German aircraft in the Thames Estuary on the very last leg of her voyage from Port Pirie. The ship went ashore on a sandbank, and was still burning three days later, although the lead ingots which made up a substantial part of her general cargo were eventually salved. Eight of her large complement of 98 were lost.

CITY OF ADELAIDE
William Gray and Co. (1918) Ltd., Wear Shipyard, Sunderland; 1920, 6589gt.

The same group included two ships named CITY OF ADELAIDE; the first of the name being torpedoed in the Mediterranean in August 1918.

All of the group came to violent ends. The second CITY OF ADELAIDE became Ellerman's final war loss when torpedoed by the Japanese submarine I-8 when bound from Karachi to Fremantle on 30th March 1944. Despite the appalling record of war crimes perpetrated by Ariizumi, the commander of this submarine, the 90 persons on board CITY OF ADELAIDE survived.

BRANKSOME HALL

Swan, Hunter and Wigham Richardson Ltd., Wallsend; 1905, 4261gt.

Along with other German shipowners, Deutsche Dampschiffahrts-Gesellchaft "Hansa" of Bremen lost all their surviving ships in 1919 as the victorious allies divided the spoils of war. Their ARENSBURG became Hall Line's BRANKSOME HALL in 1920.

A rather ignominious accident robbed her of the honour of becoming the last ship with a Hall name. On 31st May 1933 she broke adrift from her moorings off Southend and collided with the anchored sailing vessel ELSIE, which was swept bodily into Southend Pier. At 28 years old, and with so many good ships unemployed, BRANKSOME HALL was not worth repairing and was sold to Italian breakers.

CITY OF AUCKLAND

A.G. "Weser", Bremen; 1914, 8336gt.

The WEISSENFELS was built in Germany almost a decade after the ARENSBURG, but looked remarkably similar. She was bought by Ellerman from the Shipping Controller in 1921 and renamed CITY OF AUCKLAND.

Surviving the Second World War she was sold in 1947 to the Chandris group, who renamed her KARTERIA under the ownership of the Christopher Steamship Co. Ltd. of London. In 1950 she hoisted the Italian flag as STEVA for her last voyage to the breakers at La Spezia.

CITY OF CHRISTCHURCH
J.C. Tecklenborg A.G., Geestemunde; 1915, 6009gt.

The Ellerman group showed a great appetite for ex-German tonnage, probably because bargain prices were being asked for relatively low-mileage ships. The steamer ASCHENBURG, for instance, had been completed only in 1915, and the British blockade would ensure she saw little real service.

Acquired in 1921 she was given the name LORENZO, suggesting that she was intended for Ellerman's Wilson Line, although ownership was vested in Ellerman and Bucknall Steamship Co. Ltd. To bring her in line with the rest of the fleet she was renamed CITY OF CHRISTCHURCH in 1929.

She was a case of Germany destroying what she had built. On 21st March 1943, whilst en route from South Wales to Algiers during the tail end of the North African campaign, she was sunk off Portugal by bombers based in occupied France. She was abandoned without casualties and sank the next day.

CITY OF BAGDAD
J.C. Tecklenborg A.G., Geestemunde; 1919, 7501gt.

There was a grim symmetry to the career of CITY OF BAGDAD. She was ordered by D.D.G. "Hansa" but shortly after completion as GEIERFELS in 1919 she was handed over to the British as war reparations, entering City Line service in 1921.

Whilst on passage from Lourenco Marques to Hong Kong she was captured by the German raider ATLANTIS on 11th July 1940 and sunk by explosive charges, all but two of her crew of 82 surviving to be taken prisoner. The symmetry ? As GOLDENFELS the ATLANTIS had also been built for D.D.G. "Hansa".

CITY OF SALFORD
Swan, Hunter and Wigham Richardson Ltd., Wallsend; 1905, 5824gt.

CITY OF SALFORD was built for the Hamburg-Sudamerikanische D.G. as SANTA CRUZ. In August 1914 she was requisitioned by the Imperial German Navy to serve as a Sperrbrecher, or "barrier breaking vessel". Although she carried the names SPERRBRECHER 5, 7 and 8, it seems unlikely she broke many barriers or blockades.

Hall Line bought her on her surrender to Britain in 1920, initially calling her MERTON HALL until she was renamed CITY OF SALFORD in 1926. She was broken up in Scotland during 1933.

CITY OF VALENCIA
Reiherstieg Schiffswerft, Hamburg; 1908, 7329gt, 117 passengers.

One of Ellerman's most significant purchases of ex-German tonnage was the two twin screw cargo passenger ships built in 1908 for Deutsche Dampschiffahrt-Gesellschaft "Kosmos" of Hamburg. In 1921 RODA and HELUAN became CITY OF VALENCIA and CITY OF LUCKNOW, respectively.

Allocated originally to City Line Ltd., CITY OF VALENCIA soon became one of a number of ageing passenger vessels to sail on Ellerman and Bucknall's American and Indian Line. She was a victim of the depression: laid up in 1933 at Liverpool, her next voyage was to the breakers at Blyth in 1934.

CITY OF DUNEDIN
Bremer Vulkan, Vegesack, 1917, 7057gt.

The four masts of CITY OF DUNEDIN leave no doubt as to her German origins. She was completed as PORTA for Norddeutscher Lloyd A.G. of Bremen in 1917: a time when a blockaded Germany could have little use for such a fine ocean-going cargo ship.

She is seen in the Mersey during her relatively brief period with Hall Line from 1921 to 1928: in the latter year she was re-acquired by her former owners, and renamed LIPPE. Her career almost ended in April 1940 when acting as a transport for the German invasion of Norway. Trapped in Narvik Fjord, she was scuttled to avoid capture. She was salved, only to be torpedoed by H.M. Submarine SCEPTRE off Frohavet on 7th April 1944.

PATRICIA
A.G. "Vulkan", Stettin; 1899, 14466gt, 246 passengers.

This remarkable photograph shows the ex-Hamburg Amerika Linie steamer PATRICIA, owned by the Shipping Controller but managed by Ellerman Lines Ltd. and wearing their funnel: she and her sister PRETORIA were the largest passenger ships ever to do so. The North Atlantic liner had been surrendered at Hamburg in 1919, and after a few months as a United States Navy transport she was passed on to Britain. No-one wanted to buy the ageing monster, and she was broken up at Blyth in November 1921.

CRESSADO
Schiffswerft von Henry Koch, Lubeck; 1913, 1228gt.

The JRE pennant at the main shows that this photograph of CRESSADO off New Brighton was taken in the late thirties, towards the end of an eventful career. She was built in 1913 as the CRESSIDA for Adolf Kirsten of Hamburg, and ceded to Britain as reparations in 1919. Ellerman bought her in 1921, altering just two letters to achieve her new name. Ownership was vested in the Gulf of Suez Steamship Co. Ltd. of London, and management in Westcott & Laurance Lines. This Mediterranean trader ran out of Liverpool only after transfer to Ellerman and Papayanni management in 1936.

On May 8th 1942 she became a war loss, but a victim of a convoy collision rather than enemy action, sinking after colliding in the Irish Sea with H.M.S. POZARICA, a MacAndrew's fruiter converted to an anti-aircraft ship. CRESSADO was carrying general cargo from Portugal to Preston.

ASSYRIAN
Blohm und Voss, Hamburg; 1914, 3083gt.

The ASSYRIAN was very much a one-off, and not just because she was the only Ellerman ship to use this name. She was one of the first ocean-going motorships, built for the Woermann Linie as FRITZ, and fitted with a pair of her builder's two stroke diesels, one for each screw. Entering the West African service in August 1914, she was almost immediately engulfed by the First World War. When the spoils of this conflict were being divided, she was surrendered to Britain in November 1919, being bought by Ellerman a year later.

The company's first motorship, spares for her engines were said to be unavailable, and after only three years she was re-engined. The photograph shows her after she had been fitted with triple expansion steam engines.

As the commodore's ship in convoy SC 7, she was bringing general cargo from New Orleans to Liverpool when torpedoed by U-101 on 18th October 1940. She sank next day, H.M.S. LEITH taking on board the 31 survivors of the 48 on board, her complement swollen by the presence of the commodore's staff and three passengers.

CITY OF BATAVIA
Swan, Hunter and Wigham Richardson Ltd., Wallsend; 1907, 5655gt.

In a career spanning 48 years, this ship served under four flags, two of her changes being as a result of war.

Built for Roland Linie A.G. of Bremen as GANELON, she was at Antwerp in August 1914 and remained there throughout the war. Surrendered to Britain, in 1921 she became CITY OF BATAVIA first under Hall Line management and then under Ellerman and Bucknall's: a rare case of such a change. In 1938 she was sold to Italian owners and became VOLUNTAS.

In June 1940 she was at Buenos Aires when Italy declared war on Britain and France, and was seized in what was an action of doubtful legality: almost alone amongst South American nations, Argentina never declared war on, or even broke off relations with, Italy. After serving in their state-owned fleet as RIO TEUCO, she was returned to Italy in 1946 and resumed her former identity.

Having survived two wars, she was unfortunate to come to a violent end in peace time. Under her final name VOLONTA she was wrecked in fog off Ushant on 12th April 1955 during a voyage from Bona to Ghent with a cargo of iron ore.

KEELUNG
Earle's Shipbuilding and Engineering Co. Ltd., Hull; 1919, 5186gt.

This "B" class standard ship was building as WAR WALRUS when taken over by the group in 1919: note the lattice derricks. She retained her original Ellerman and Bucknall name KEELUNG unusually late, not becoming CITY OF KEELUNG until 1936.

Sold out of the fleet in 1947, she went to a London Greek who registered her in Hong Kong as HELLENIC TRADER. In 1951 she became NICHIAN MARU, a name she still carried when she arrived at Shimizu for scrap in 1960.

CITY OF CHRISTIANIA
Earle's Shipbuilding and Engineering Co. Ltd., Hull; 1921, 4940gt.

The long fo'c'sle design introduced during the First World War became a standard feature of the Hall Line fleet in post war years, with nine turbine steamers built to this layout between 1920 and 1925. One of the longest lived of this class was CITY OF CHRISTIANIA, which was only broken up on the Tyne in 1957 at the age of 36.

CITY OF EVANSVILLE
William Gray and Co. Ltd., West Hartlepool; 1922, 6558gt.

CITY OF EVANSVILLE was built to much the same design as CITY OF CHRISTIANIA give or take a few variations introduced by her builder. The group introduced some new names to the Ellerman group, although few were as obscure as CITY OF EVANSVILLE: neither of the settlements of that name in Indiana or Wisconsin being of any significance.

Her war seems to have been fairly uneventful, and her most notable service was carrying some very large human cargoes. After the fall of France in 1940 she carried 1,500 French troops to Morocco for repatriation. As if this experience was not enough for her long-suffering officers and crew, she returned from North Africa with a similar number of British refugees. In 1957 she was sold to a Panama-flag subsidiary of Wallem and Co. Ltd. of Hong Kong and renamed DOREA, being broken up at Keelung in 1958.

CITY LINERS OF THE TWENTIES

CITY OF CAMBRIDGE
Workman, Clark and Co. Ltd., Belfast; 1921, 7056gt.

CITY OF CAMBRIDGE was one of the last City Line ships to be completed with a black hull, and seems to have retained this colour longer than her running mates who began to be painted grey in 1921.

She became one of the relatively few casualties which the large Ellerman fleet sustained during the thirties. On 6th October 1934 she stranded on the Pratas Reef in the South China Sea, not far from the end of her voyage to Hong Kong from New York, San Francisco and Manila. Few wrecks are peaceful, but before the end of the year the CITY OF CAMBRIDGE suffered the indignity of being looted and burnt.

CITY OF SIMLA
William Gray and Co. (1918) Ltd., West Hartlepool; 1921, 9468gt.

This turbine steamer was mainly employed on City Line's Indian service, but was also used on the Ellerman and Bucknall routes to South Africa when need arose.

Almost inevitably for a ship of her period, she was a war loss; sunk off Northern Ireland on 21st September 1940 when the German submarine U-138 wrought havoc on her convoy. She was outward bound from the Clyde to Bombay via the Cape, and remarkably there were only three losses from her large complement of 183 crew and 167 passengers.

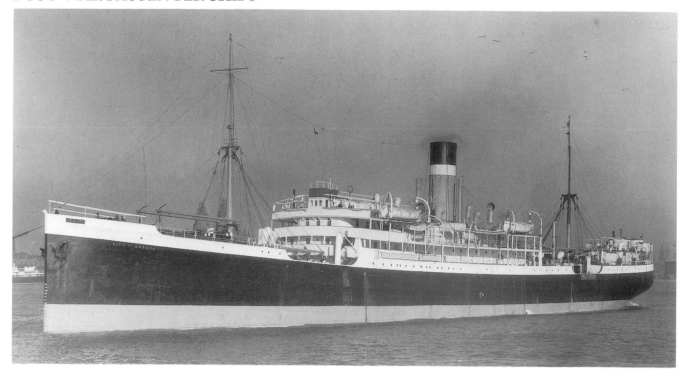

CITY OF BARODA
Barclay, Curle and Co. Ltd., Glasgow; 1918, 6719gt, 113 passengers.

Although Ellermans adopted dove grey hulls soon after the First World War, some Hall Line vessels such as the CITY OF BARODA retained black hulls well into the thirties. She was laid down as a pure cargo carrier but completed as a passenger ship, the last for Hall Line's traditional Calcutta route.

Like many of her generation, CITY OF BARODA was a victim of U-boat attack, torpedoed by U-509 on 2nd April 1943 soon after she had left Walvis Bay. Following the attack she went ashore at Luderitz on the coast of South West Africa and quickly broke up, although fortunately losses were relatively light, with only 13 casualties out of the 303 aboard. At the time she was on a circuitous voyage with general cargo and mail from London to India via Trinidad and South Africa.

CITY OF CANTERBURY
Swan, Hunter and Wigham Richardson Ltd., Wallsend; 1922, 8421gt, 168 passengers.

City Line's CITY OF CANTERBURY was very much an "intermediate" ship, for which read small and slow compared with contemporaries like CITY OF PARIS: she carried her passengers at a sedate 13 knots. In 1930 her speed and her time-keeping were improved by the addition of exhaust turbines to her quadruple expansion engines.

Few merchant ships can have survived such varied war service as CITY OF CANTERBURY. As a troop transport she helped to garrison and then to evacuate Crete, experienced a near-mutiny at Durban whilst taking troops to Singapore immediately before its fall, spent several years in a far from peaceful Mediterranean, and made a number of trips to the Normandy beaches. Normal service for City Line was not resumed until 1947, reconditioning by her builder giving her another six years' service. She was broken up at Blyth in 1953.

CITY OF PARIS
Swan, Hunter and Wigham Richardson Ltd., Wallsend; 1922, 10902gt, 333 passengers.

The turbine steamer CITY OF PARIS probably had more adventures under Ellerman ownership than any other ship. These began before she was finished, as due to a shipyard strike she was taken to St. Nazaire for completion.

The first photograph shows her with her original black hull and was probably taken before 1924. Thereafter she took a number of cruises in Ellerman's Wilson Line colours, and when returned to City Line was given a grey hull. A spell of inactivity followed when laid up in the thirties, but she later switched to Ellerman and Bucknall's South African service.

War was quick to bring her new experiences: during September 1939 she struck one of the first magnetic mines. Later trooping duties were slightly less hazardous, although she narrowly missed being at Singapore when it fell to the Japanese. Conversion to a headquarters ship was started but not finished, and she then served as an accommodation ship at Hong Kong before resuming work as a trooper. When returned to Ellermans in 1947 she was extensively rebuilt, as shown in the second photograph, and returned to the South African service. She was finally made redundant by the CITY OF PORT ELIZABETH class, and was broken up at Newport in 1956.

CITY OF HONGKONG

Earle's Shipbuilding and Engineering Co. Ltd., Hull; 1924, 9678gt, 104 passengers.

Although both the beginning and end of her life were somewhat traumatic, CITY OF HONGKONG had a very successful career with the Ellerman group.

She was laid down in 1923 as the cargo ship COLORADO for Ellerman's Wilson Line, but redesigned to carry passengers for City Line. Within a few years of completion she was seconded to Ellerman and Bucknall's routes, as seen in the upper photograph. Note that she is still registered at Hull: a sign of her Wilson parentage. For South African services her original quadruple expansion engines proved somewhat under-powered, and she had an exhaust turbine added in 1930, giving a modest increase in speed. The second photograph shows her after returning to City Line service in 1936; she had now lost her forward pair of kingposts.

Surviving her war service as a troopship, she was sold in 1951 to the Italian Grimaldi company, who renamed her CENTAURO for services to South America, although she also ran on the North Atlantic. On one such voyage in February 1955 she called at Bermuda for bunkers, lost her anchors and ran aground. Although refloated she was too old to be worth repairing and was broken up later that year at Savona.

CITY OF VENICE
Workman, Clark and Co. Ltd., Belfast; 1924, 8308gt, 165 passengers.

Oddly, whilst pure cargo carriers for the group were being given turbines, City Line's passenger ship CITY OF VENICE had to make do with quadruple expansion engines, which pushed her stately frame along at 14 knots. In 1932 her machinery was updated with the fitting of a low pressure exhaust turbine.

Her reputation for slowness seemed to stay with her until the end. As part of the assault force for Operation Torch - the landings in Sicily - she was allocated to a slow convoy, and entrusted largely with motor transport. Creeping along the North African coast at eight knots she was a relatively easy target for U-375, which torpedoed her and the accompanying ST. ESSYLT on 4th July 1943.

CITY OF BENARES
Barclay, Curle and Co. Ltd., Glasgow; 1936, 11081gt, 219 passengers.

The tragedy of her sinking has clouded memories of the second CITY OF BENARES, and it tends to be forgotten that in her day she was a particularly notable ship. She was the only passenger ship built for Ellermans in the thirties, City Line's largest and fastest ship, and the only two-funnelled ship the group ever owned.

Much has been written of her sinking by U-48 on 17th September 1940 during a voyage from Liverpool to Montreal. What has not been fully explained is the folly which sent a ship carrying 191 passengers and which was capable of 17 knots out into the Atlantic in an unescorted, eight-knot convoy. Of the 406 aboard, 261 were lost, including almost all of the 90 child evacuees.

PALMELLA
Ramage and Ferguson Ltd., Leith; 1920, 1568gt.

The PALMELLA makes the point that not all Ellerman and Papayanni ships carried names ending -IAN.

Her career followed a pattern which becomes depressingly familiar. After two decades' service she was torpedoed off Portugal on 1st December 1940, whilst on a voyage to Oporto with a cargo including sacks of mail for prisoners-of-war. The culprit was U-37, but fortunately all but one of PALMELLA's complement survived.

ESTRELLANO
Hall, Russell and Co. Ltd., Aberdeen; 1920, 1963gt.

ESTRELLANO, contemporary of PALMELLA, was sunk by the same U-boat. On 9th February 1941 she was torpedoed off Portugal whilst homeward bound in a Gibraltar convoy. Six of her crew of 26 were lost.

EGYPTIAN
W. Harkess and Son Ltd., Middlesbrough; 1920, 2866gt.

This classic view shows the third EGYPTIAN with just enough way on to stem the Mersey tide. Her name is a reminder of John Ellerman's first venture into shipping, when in 1892 he was part of a syndicate which bought the fleet of Frederick Leyland and Co., of which the oldest ship was the EGYPTIAN.

The EGYPTIAN's end came in mid-Atlantic on 6th March 1943, torpedoed by the German submarine U-230 with the loss of all but three of her complement of 47. As part of convoy SC 121 she was on the final leg of a voyage from Lagos to Loch Ewe via New York.

DIDO
Dunlop, Bremner and Co. Ltd., Port Glasgow; 1920, 3554gt.

The DIDO had, quite literally, more than her share of ups and downs, being sunk on at least three occasions and seriously stranded once. Completed for Ellerman's Wilson Line Ltd., in 1929 she was transferred to Ellerman and Papayanni management.

Her adventures began in September 1939 when she rescued over 200 of the crew of the aircraft carrier H.M.S. COURAGEOUS, torpedoed west of Ireland. In May 1940 DIDO stranded off Ushant in fog, and when refloated was taken into Brest for dry-docking. It was not a good place to be immobilised, and as France fell she was abandoned by her crew. Following the formalities of condemning her as a prize, the Germans took her over in April 1941 as a naval auxiliary. As DORPAT she was sunk by a mine off Aarhus in April 1943, but was refloated. Whilst she was under repair at Aalborg the Danish resistance succeeded in sinking her with bombs, but by November 1944 she had been returned to service. In May 1945 she was sunk yet again, this time by Allied aircraft in the Langeland Belt. Although she was refloated, Ellermans were not interested in having her back, and after four years' idleness she was sold in 1949 to Finnish owners who renamed her LEILA. She lasted until 1963, when broken up in Finland.

ALGERIAN
Barclay, Curle and Co. Ltd., Glasgow; 1924, 2305gt.

During the course of a long career ALGERIAN had a most unusual job. In 1943 she was taken over by the Admiralty and equipped to lay the "Pipe Line Under The Ocean" to supply fuel to the Normandy beachhead. She was returned to Ellerman in 1946, and served until broken up in 1957. The photograph was taken in October 1938.

LANCASTRIAN
Palmer's Shipbuilding and Iron Co. Ltd., Jarrow; 1924, 2996gt.

Although spending her career on Ellerman and Papayanni's Mediterranean service, LANCASTRIAN was known for most of her life as CITY OF LANCASTER, only being renamed in 1947. She is seen here in April 1950.

Her war service was eventful: by a grim coincidence she was lying near Cunard's LANCASTRIA when the latter sank with heavy loss of life during the evacuation of France.

LANCASTRIAN was broken up at Troon in 1953.

CITY OF OXFORD
Swan, Hunter and Wigham Richardson Ltd., Wallsend; 1926, 2759gt.

Sometimes the only way of telling for which company an Ellerman ship was running was by looking at her houseflag. The name of the CITY OF OXFORD reflects her ownership by Ellerman Lines Ltd., but her size suggests she was built for Ellerman and Papayanni Lines' Mediterranean trades. However, she did not come under the management of the latter company until 1936. Her end came when sunk by U-552 off the Azores on 15th June 1942, with the loss of only one of her complement of 44. She was homeward bound from Lisbon to Garston with ore and cork in her holds.

BELGRAVIAN
William Gray and Co. Ltd., West Hartlepool; 1937, 3136gt.

The BELGRAVIAN of 1937 was the second of a group of six ships which helped to renew the fleet of the Ellerman and Papayanni Line as trade improved in the late thirties. They were elegant small cargo liners whose general design was to become familiar in the post-war fleet. Another feature to be adopted by other Ellerman ships was the deep white upper strake to her hull.

Only two ships of this group were to survive the war. BELGRAVIAN was the last of the four to be lost, sunk on 6th August 1941, the day after she had been torpedoed by the German submarine U-372. She was returning to Hull from Port Harcourt and Freetown with a cargo of ground nuts and tin ore, when convoy SL 81 was attacked by a wolf pack in the Atlantic west of Ireland. Two were lost out of her crew of fifty, which today seems an enormous complement for a ship of her modest size.

CITY OF DERBY
William Gray and Co.(1918) Ltd., Sunderland; 1921, 6616gt.

The requirements of radio reception led to all Ellerman ships featuring high topmasts in the twenties, but the long yardarms fitted to the CITY OF DERBY were unusual. Completed as KARONGA for Ellerman and Bucknall, only in 1927 was she given a City name as rules on nomenclature were tightened up.

As CITY OF DERBY she served her owners for thirty years, and even then could find a buyer. In February 1957 the Fairtrade Steamship Co. Ltd. purchased her, and got two further years' work out of her as the Liberian FAIRTRADE before she was broken up at Kobe.

CITY OF WINDSOR
Wear Shipyard Ltd., Sunderland; 1923, 7247gt.

The Ellerman group explored almost every possible variation in positioning of six hatches, but KNARESBRO' was unique in having two on the bridge deck aft of the engine room.

Renamed CITY OF WINDSOR in 1928, she went on to have an unusually full war. She helped to evacuate troops from Cherbourg in June 1940 and from Greece just a year later, both under heavy air attack. Putting troops ashore, as she did in the Persian Gulf and later at the Salerno landings, must have come as a welcome change. Released from requisition early, she was returned to Ellerman and Bucknall in 1944, and steamed on until broken up at Briton Ferry in 1953.

CITY OF KIMBERLEY
William Gray and Co. Ltd., West Hartlepool; 1925, 6204gt.

The CITY OF KIMBERLEY of 1925 was the first ship built new for the Ellerman and Bucknall Steamship Co. Ltd. with a City name, although some purchased ships had previously been renamed in the Ellerman style.

Her career was long, relatively peaceful and, one trusts, profitable. She continued under Ellerman and Bucknall ownership until 1960, when sold to the Argonaut Shipping and Trading Co. Ltd. who placed her under the Liberian flag as FAIRHURST. She was almost immediately resold to the People's Republic of China, but Lloyd's Register does not suggest she was renamed. On 5th September 1964, whilst heading for the breakers at Shanghai, she broke loose from her tow during a gale shortly after leaving Hong Kong and was wrecked.

CITY OF CANBERRA
William Gray and Co. Ltd., West Hartlepool; 1927, 7485gt.

Names such as CITY OF CANBERRA given to Ellerman and Bucknall ships reflected the worldwide nature of the company's routes: a service from Manchester and Liverpool to Australia and New Zealand via the Panama Canal being started well before the CITY OF CANBERRA was built.

She finished her career in an Inverkeithing scrapyard in 1957.

CITY OF MANDALAY
Swan, Hunter and Wigham Richardson Ltd., Wallsend; 1925, 7049gt.

Note how the omission of the deep white strake which was usual for Ellerman ships gives CITY OF MANDALAY a rather dour appearance. She was managed by W.S. Workman, which indicated that she was destined for City Line service. She also served Ellerman and Bucknall routes whilst, just to complicate matters, in this photograph she is flying Hall Line's houseflag.

On 17th October 1939 she had the misfortune to become the first of the 83 ships which the group lost during the war. Whilst standing by Bibby's YORKSHIRE, which had been torpedoed by U-46, CITY OF MANDALAY was sunk by the same submarine, one of four which attacked convoy HG3. There were seven survivors from CITY OF MANDALAY, which was on passage from the Far East to Europe.

CITY OF DELHI
Wear Shipyard of William Gray and Co. Ltd., Sunderland; 1925, 7443gt.

The Ellerman group stayed faithful to steam reciprocating machinery when others were flirting with diesels. By the time the CITY OF DELHI was delivered steam machinery had reached a high level of sophistication. The builder's Central Marine Engine Works fitted her with quadruple expansion engines with an exhaust turbine, which meant that the steam was used four times in successive cylinders, and any expansive power it still had was then used to turn a turbine coupled to the main shaft.

Despite this sophisticated machinery her speed is recorded as an unexciting twelve and a half knots. But what she lacked in knots she made up for in mileage, and she was broken up at Bo'ness in 1957 after steaming along for over thirty years.

CITY OF DURBAN
Earle's Shipbuilding and Engineering Co. Ltd., Hull; 1921, 4499gt.

Shipbuilders Earle's of Hull had been acquired by the Wilson family in 1901, and were not sold to Ellerman with the family's shipping interests. Nevertheless, the yard supplied several vessels to companies in the group. The CITY OF DURBAN appears to have been taken over for Hall Line management whilst on the stocks. Turbines were beginning to be fitted to cargo liners at this time, and the CITY OF DURBAN received three of them.

During the twenties Ellerman ships were not always named appropriately for their intended trade, but the group became more particular with its nomenclature after the Second World War. When a quartet of passenger liners was ordered for the South Africa service the name CITY OF DURBAN was wanted, and so in 1952 the cargo ship became CITY OF GLOUCESTER. As this she gave a little over five years' further service before being broken up at Briton Ferry.

CITY OF DUNDEE
Palmer's Shipbuilding and Iron Co. Ltd., Jarrow; 1921, 5270gt.

Robert Alexander first used a Hall name for his iron ship HADDON HALL of 1868. This naming scheme, which gave rise to both the unofficial and later the official name of his company, was last used in 1921 for the SANDON HALL. When most parts of the group standardised on City names in 1926, she became the CITY OF DUNDEE. She lasted until 1957 when she was broken up at Port Glasgow.

CITY OF BEDFORD
William Gray and Co. Ltd., Wear Shipyard, Sunderland; 1924, 6407gt.

In 1924, two outwardly similar cargo ships were delivered to the Hall Line, the CITY OF SALISBURY and the CITY OF BEDFORD, seen here. Internally there was a major difference, however: the CITY OF SALISBURY made do with triple expansion machinery whilst her near sister had quadruple expansion engines.

CITY OF BEDFORD was a victim of war, although not of hostile action, colliding with the Elder, Dempster motor vessel BODNANT south of Iceland on 30th December 1940. She was in a homeward convoy from New York and Halifax, and amongst her general cargo were several million rifle cartridges. Prime Minister Churchill directed ascerbic remarks at the Admiralty on the folly of not splitting such a badly needed consignment of ammunition between more than one ship.

CITY OF BATH
William Gray and Co. Ltd., West Hartlepool; 1926, 5079gt.

As the ships on this page bear witness, a large proportion of Ellerman ships from the twenties failed to survive the war. The CITY OF BATH was torpedoed off Trinidad by U-508 early on the morning of 2nd December 1942 with the loss of six lives. She was on a voyage from Mombasa to the United Kingdom via Pernambuco with copper and ore.

CITY OF ROUBAIX *see opposite*

CITY OF HEREFORD (*above*), **INCHONA** (*below*)
Barclay, Curle and Co. Ltd., Glasgow; 1927, 5101gt.

Twenty or thirty years separate these two photographs, years which the CITY OF HEREFORD seems to have weathered well. The second photograph shows her during the period from 1955 to 1956 when the Hong Kong-based Williamson and Co. ran her as INCHONA. She was still good for further trading, and as the Hong Kong-owned GOLDEN ALPHA was broken up at Osaka during 1959.

CITY OF ROUBAIX (*opposite*)
Swan, Hunter and Wigham Richardson Ltd., Wallsend; 1928, 7108gt.

Occasionally the Ellerman group chose some obscure cities, or perhaps they were towns, after which to name their ships. The turbine steamer CITY OF ROUBAIX took her title from a settlement in Nord Department of France, near Lille. Her sister was named CITY OF LYONS; there was a contemporary CITY OF LILLE but as an accompanying photograph shows, she was only distantly related.

She was to be another fine cargo liner lost during the abortive attempt to avert the fall of Greece. On 6th April 1941 she survived an air raid in Piraeus, but was less fortunate next day when the CLAN FRASER was hit and blew up, setting fire to the CITY OF ROUBAIX. With 50 tons of explosives amongst her military stores, she exploded, broke in two and sank. Remarkably, according to official figures there were no casualties amongst her complement of 95.

CITY OF LILLE

Barclay, Curle and Co. Ltd., Glasgow; 1928, 6583gt.

After experience with the ASSYRIAN, Ellermans showed some reluctance to adopt diesel engines. The CITY OF LILLE was the first motorship ordered by the group, but whilst her Doxford opposed piston engines seem to have been remarkably trouble-free, she was not repeated.

CITY OF LILLE motored on under Hall Line management for almost 30 years. Even then she could find a buyer from Taiwan: China Union Lines getting another six years' work out of her as UNION CAPITOL under their own and the Liberian flag, before breaking her up in Taiwan in 1963.

CITY OF DIEPPE

William Gray and Co. Ltd., West Hartlepool; 1929, 7560gt.

City Line's CITY OF DIEPPE was another subject of an apparently successful experiment which was not repeated. In 1934 she was lengthened and fitted with a Maier bow which increased her speed from 14 to 16 knots. In spite of this, the bow design was not incorporated into any subsequent Ellerman ships.

CITY OF DIEPPE survived her war service, at least part of which she spent as a store ship at Freetown, Sierra Leone - a wasteful, sedentary role for fast, modern ship. Ellerman service ended in 1956 with her sale to become the EASTMAN under Bahamas registry. She was broken up at Hong Kong in 1959.

CITY OF BARCELONA *see opposite*

CITY OF SYDNEY
Workman, Clark and Co. (1928) Ltd., Belfast; 1930, 6986gt.

CITY OF SYDNEY's triple expansion engines with low pressure turbines were supplied by oil-fired boilers: an innovation which reportedly saved eight firemen, but was not widely adopted by the Ellerman group until after the war.

During a long career, her moment of greatest glory came during her last voyage for Ellerman. In March 1958 she took on board 1,300 passengers from the Norwegian emigrant ship SKAUBRYN, on fire in the Indian Ocean. This complement was far in excess of the number she could feed or comfortably accommodate, and they were quickly transferred to an Italian liner. The CITY OF SYDNEY was sold to the Tsavliris group two months later, and ran briefly as NICOLAOS TSAVLIRIS under the Greek flag until broken up at Hong Kong in 1960.

CITY OF MANCHESTER
Cammell, Laird and Co. Ltd., Birkenhead; 1935, 8917gt.

CITY OF MANCHESTER was a particularly modern looking ship; she had a profile that would not have disgraced a ship built twenty years later.

Her career with Hall Line was to be tragically short. On 28th February 1942, shortly after leaving Java, she was sunk by torpedo and gunfire from the Japanese submarine I-153. Of her enormous complement of 137, three were lost and six were presumed to have been taken prisoner.

CITY OF BARCELONA *(opposite)*
Barclay, Curle and Co. Ltd., Glasgow; 1930, 5698gt.

The clumsy-looking gear around the foremast of the CITY OF BARCELONA supports her heavy lift gear. Its capacity of 30 tons was considered notable at the time, but seems modest: Hall Line must have loaded locomotives and other heavy items weighing several times this figure.

CITY OF BARCELONA was a case of design taking one step back, and her counter stern makes her look dated compared with contemporary cargo liners. She survived the war and was broken up at Antwerp in 1958.

CITY OF AGRA
William Denny and Bros. Ltd., Dumbarton; 1936, 6361gt.

Placing her third hatch on the bridge deck forward of the accommodation gave CITY OF AGRA a profile which was unique in the Ellerman fleet, although many Blue Funnel ships were later built to this design. Completed for Hall Line, CITY OF AGRA was turbine driven but coal fired: something of an expensive anachronism in terms of the firemen needed. Despite this she had a long career, going to breakers at Bilbao only in 1965.

CITY OF KARACHI
Barclay, Curle and Co. Ltd., Glasgow; 1937, 7140gt.

Barclay, Curle contributed two 15 knot turbine steamers to Hall Line's fleet in the late thirties: CITY OF BOMBAY and CITY OF KARACHI, the latter being transferred to City Line management. Sadly, both were to be war losses. On 13th April 1941 CITY OF KARACHI was damaged by aircraft during the ill-starred operations in Crete. Despite being beached a day later, she was attacked further and was completely wrecked. Although there were no casualties amongst her complement of 103, official sources record that "35 native crew were sent to the hills, and may have been taken prisoner".

CITY OF CAPETOWN CLASS

CITY OF LINCOLN
Cammell Laird and Co. Ltd., Birkenhead; 1938, 8039gt.

Standardisation was the order of the day in the late thirties, and with trade improving five ships were ordered; the first major Ellerman order to go to Birkenhead. The CITY OF CAPE TOWN class were twin screw turbine steamers capable of 14 knots, but - despite the success of CITY OF SYDNEY - all were coal-fired. The CITY OF LINCOLN was the second of the class delivered to Ellerman and Bucknall.

She survived the war, only to come to grief on the South African coast near Cape Agulhas on 9th November 1946. Salvage took four months, and she was then taken to Cape Town where her general cargo destined for India was unloaded, and the ship herself was slowly stripped. Her end did not come until May 1950, when the scuttling of her remains gave the South African Air Force an opportunity for some target practice.

CITY OF EDINBURGH
Cammell Laird and Co. Ltd., Birkenhead; 1938, 8036gt.

Completed for City Line management, the CITY OF EDINBURGH was the third of the CITY OF CAPE TOWN class and was to have the most adventurous war of the class. In 1943 she was requisitioned by the Admiralty for conversion to a landing ship headquarters, and given the rather appropriate name H.M.S. LOTHIAN - one of the few successes of what became a rather farcical affair. Not long after D-day, and still incomplete, she set out for the Pacific as headquarters ship for a British force of landing ships which was intended to link up with the U.S. 7th Fleet. With a total of 750 on board, the overcrowding gave rise to an armed mutiny on the way. When she eventually arrived at New Guinea the U.S. Navy took no interest in her, and she saw little if any action.

After return to Ellermans in 1946 she was reconditioned and transferred to the management of the Ellerman and Bucknall Steamship Co. Ltd. In 1961 she was sold and renamed CASTLE MOUNT for a last voyage to Hong Kong and the breakers.

SAMARINA *(above)*, **CITY OF ELY** *(below)*
Bethlehem-Fairfield Shipyard Inc., Baltimore; 1943, 7258gt.

SAMARINA is seen in the upper photograph arriving at a misty Liverpool in May 1947, the only colour on the grey ship being her Ellerman funnel. The group managed a number of Liberties for the Ministry of War Transport, who bareboat chartered them from the United States War Shipping Administration, for whom SAMARINA had been launched as JAMES BLAIR.

After the war a dozen of these Liberties were bought and scattered across the group; SAMARINA becoming CITY OF ELY under Ellerman and Bucknall ownership in 1947. The lower photograph of her taken in 1948 suggests she was less well cared for than other Ellerman ships.

Lives of group Liberties varied; CITY OF ELY having one of the longest, being sold in 1961. As the British-flag PAGET TRADER she tramped for a few years until laid up following a cargo fire. She was demolished at Kaohsiung in 1966.

CITY OF CHELMSFORD
Bethlehem-Fairfield Shipyard Inc., Baltimore; 1943, 7271gt.

Ellerman and Bucknall took more than their share of the Liberty steamers, several of which were given East Anglian place names. CITY OF CHELMSFORD had been launched as LIONEL COPLEY, and was then renamed SAMBRAKE for charter to Britain.

When sold in 1959 her Panamanian owners considered her worth investing in, and had her fitted with a diesel engine at Newport in South Wales. As the Greek-owned SAN GEORGE and later SUERTE she motored on under the Lebanese and Greek flags until broken up in Yugoslavia in 1971.

EMPIRE SPARTAN
Lithgows Ltd., Port Glasgow; 1942, 7009gt.

Seen here in August 1947, EMPIRE SPARTAN is still in war rig and with narrow funnel, yet managers Ellerman and Bucknall have painted her in their livery. They bought her from the Ministry of Transport and renamed her CITY OF CARDIFF in 1951. She was sold after just eight years, and as the Hong Kong-owned SHUN WING steamed on until broken up at Kaohsiung in 1972.

CITY OF BRISTOL
Swan, Hunter and Wigham Richardson Ltd., Wallsend; 1943, 8424gt.

Despite much standardisation in shipbuilding during the Second World War, many cargo liners were completed to owners' plans. Ellerman had a modest three ships built, but still managed to produce a new design, with little in common with either the pre-war CITY OF CAPETOWN or CITY OF KARACHI classes. First of the group was the turbine-driven CITY OF BRISTOL for City Line. She lasted in the Ellerman fleet only until 1961, when she was sold to owners in Formosa and became TUNG LEE. Kaohsiung breakers demolished her in 1963.

CITY OF SWANSEA
Barclay, Curle and Co. Ltd., Glasgow; 1946, 9959gt.

Malta convoys and other operations having proven the value of fast, well-equipped ships, the emergency shipbuilding programme shifted from quantity to quality in the later stages of the Second World War with a group of fifteen-knot cargo liners. Ellerman took six of these; Hall Line's CITY OF SWANSEA being an example with Doxford diesels.

In 1968 three of this group were bought by Ben Line Steamers Ltd. of Leith. CITY OF SWANSEA was renamed BENKITLAN, and gave her new owners four years of service before going to a Kaohsiung scrapyard in 1972.

CITY OF POONA (above), BENARKLE (below)
Swan, Hunter and Wigham Richardson Ltd., Wallsend; 1946, 9962gt.

Hall Line's CITY OF POONA was a twin to the CITY OF SWANSEA, and the sisters' careers were almost identical. She too was sold to Ben Line in 1968, becoming BENARKLE, as shown in the lower photograph. Although delayed by two years, her fate was also at the hands of Kaohsiung breakers, to whom she was sold in 1974.

CITY OF LONDON
Swan, Hunter and Wigham Richardson Ltd., Wallsend; 1947, 8434gt.

CITY OF LONDON is dressed overall for the Coronation Review at Spithead in June 1953: note the Ellerman and Bucknall houseflag flown at her foremast rather than its usual position at the mainmast head. She was one of four twin screw turbine steamers split between the Ellerman and Bucknall and Hall Line fleets.

She was sold early in 1967, and as the Greek-owned SANDRA N ran for almost two years before arriving at Kaohsiung for demolition right at the end of 1968.

CITY OF PRETORIA
Cammell Laird and Co. Ltd., Birkenhead; 1947, 8450gt.

Although not on review, CITY OF PRETORIA looks as smart as her sister CITY OF LONDON. CITY OF PRETORIA was also sold by Ellerman and Bucknall in 1967, but made just one more voyage to the breakers in Japan under the Panama flag as PROXENEION.

CITY OF JOHANNESBURG
Barclay, Curle and Co. Ltd., Glasgow; 1947, 8207gt.

In what became a rather uniform fleet in post-war years, Hall Line's CITY OF JOHANNESBURG stood out. Intended to be the fifth member of the CITY OF NEW YORK class, she was completed as a motor vessel; her squat funnel giving her a distinctive outline. Her Ellerman service spanned 23 years, her diesels ensuring a longer life span than most of her steam contemporaries. In 1970 she went to Greek owners as FILOTHEI and then LYKAVITOS, lasting until 1973 when broken up at Kaohsiung.

CITY OF BATH
Blythswood Shipbuilding Co. Ltd., Glasgow; 1947, 6869gt.

Ellerman and Bucknall's diesel-engined CITY OF BATH was a rare acquisition from other owners. She was completed in June 1947 for the Medomsley Steam Shipping Co. Ltd. as LANGLEESCOT. Bought in 1952, she sailed as CITY OF BATH until 1969, after which she spent three years under the Cypriot flag as LENA before being broken up at Castellon, Spain in 1972.

ANGLIAN
William Gray and Co. Ltd., West Hartlepool; 1947, 2219gt.

The triple expansion machinery of the ANGLIAN was a questionable choice for a Mediterranean trader, which would visit many ports during a round voyage: a diesel would have been much quicker to start when needing to get underway.

Her steam engines probably contributed to the early sale of the ANGLIAN: in 1963 she went out to the South African coast to serve as BULWARK. After 1968 she became first the Hong Kong-owned AROMA and later the Taiwan-owned FROMA, both under the Panama flag, before being broken up in 1973.

CITY OF LEEDS
Joseph L. Thompson and Sons Ltd., Sunderland; 1947, 3518gt.

The Ellerman and Papayanni fleet had suffered as badly as other parts of the group during the war, but there were no suitable war-built vessels to act as replacements. The rebuilding programme got underway with turbine steamers which externally had a lot in common with the last pre-war class built for Ellerman and Papayanni: compare the photograph of BELGRAVIAN.

The VENETIAN of this group is seen here as Ellerman and Bucknall's CITY OF LEEDS, which she became in 1964. This renaming was a taste of things to come; after her sale in 1965 she became the Liberian CATERINA P and later the Greek TRANSRODOPI III. In 1968 she hoisted the Bulgarian flag as ACRUX and then SILISTRA. She was broken up at Split in 1976.

LUCIAN
William Gray and Co. Ltd., West Hartlepool; 1948, 1516gt.

Contemporary with ANGLIAN and VENETIAN, Ellerman and Papayanni also had this class of small motorships built for the United Kingdom to Portugal service. There cannot have been many companies simultaneously accepting ships driven by diesel, turbine and steam reciprocating engines.

LUCIAN was the third of the motorships, and like her sisters was distinguished at times by a white hull. In 1964 she became the first of the class to be sold, but notched up another 16 year's service as the Greek-owned AMORGOS and YASHOO. She was broken up as GULF STAR in 1980.

MERCIAN
Swan, Hunter and Wigham Richardson Ltd., Wallsend; 1948, 1516gt.

MERCIAN had most of her adventures after leaving Ellerman and Papayanni service in 1970. She carried a variety of names: RINOULA, GABRIELLA and DONATELLA 1 under the Cypriot and Panama flags, and STABIA 1 for Italian owners. Under the last name she was wrecked at Salerno on 4th January 1979 when arriving from Brazil: a long voyage for a small ship.

PALMELIAN
Henry Robb Ltd., Leith; 1948, 1533gt.

The PALMELIAN's career started embarrassingly when she was launched as PAMELIAN. Putting this right was the only renaming she was subject to, and when retired from Ellerman and Papayanni service in 1970 she went directly to Bilbao for scrap.

CITY OF OXFORD CLASS

CITY OF OXFORD (top left)
John Brown and Co. Ltd., Clydebank; 1948, 7593gt.

A large class of turbine steamers built soon after the war virtually defined the appearance of the City and Hall Line fleets in the fifties and sixties. The first completed was CITY OF OXFORD for City Line of Glasgow, built appropriately by a Clydeside yard.

Relatively fast turbine steamers were not particularly popular with flag-of-convenience owners, and few of this class had long lives after leaving the fleet. Sold in 1976, CITY OF OXFORD worked for Taiwanese owners for just two years as the UNION ARABIA before being demolished at Kaohsiung.

CITY OF PERTH (top right)
Caledon Shipbuilding and Engineering Co. Ltd., Dundee; 1949, 7547gt.

The CITY OF PERTH found a buyer when her career with City Line ended in 1967, but came to grief less than two months later. On her first voyage as ELENI F she was beached near Alexandria after striking a wreck.

CITY OF LEEDS (centre right), **GULF VENTURE** (bottom right)
Vickers-Armstrongs Ltd., Newcastle; 1950, 7622gt.

Last of the class was Hall Line's CITY OF OTTAWA. She was intended to be CITY OF GUILDFORD, but the logic which saw her launched with a Canadian name was reversed in 1971 when she became CITY OF LEEDS, as seen here.

The aerial view shows her after her sale in 1975, when she retained her British registry as GULF VENTURE. Ultimate owners were Gulf Shipping Lines Ltd., a large organisation which at various times had interests in London, Hong Kong and Pakistan. GULF VENTURE arrived at Gadani Beach to be broken up late in 1977.

CITY OF BROOKLYN (bottom left)
Swan, Hunter and Wigham Richardson Ltd., Wallsend; 1949, 7557gt.

CITY OF BROOKLYN was the first of the class for Hall Line, having been laid down as CITY OF GLOUCESTER. She was also one of shortest lived, becoming the Greek LEFKADIOS in 1967. As this she was abandoned by her crew on 27th September 1970 when she caught fire in the Indian Ocean during a voyage from Bordeaux to Shanghai.

CITY OF BEDFORD

Alexander Stephen and Sons Ltd., Linthouse; 1950, 7341gt.

Split superstructure went out of fashion after the CITY OF OXFORD class, and the next Ellerman newbuildings had a much tidier appearance. Note the particularly large funnel of Hall Line's CITY OF BEDFORD; other members of the class, as in the lower photograph, had large pipes added to improve smoke dispersal.

After 22 years' service CITY OF BEDFORD was sold to Spanish breakers, spared the indignity of working out her declining years under flags of convenience.

CITY OF SINGAPORE

Alexander Stephen and Sons Ltd., Linthouse; 1951, 7338gt

Hall Line had good service from all three turbine steamers of this class, and CITY OF SINGAPORE was sold only in 1975. The same owners who had bought CITY OF OTTAWA then purchased her, running her as UNITED MARINER and then GULF MARINER until she was broken up at Gadani Beach in 1977.

CITY OF BRISBANE

Cammell, Laird and Co. Ltd., Birkenhead; 1951, 10596gt.

As well as taking several ships of the standard classes built for the group post-war, Ellerman and Bucknall also built ships to its own design. Particularly large funnels distinguished two turbine steamers, the first of which was the CITY OF BRISBANE. It was still a time of indecision over names, and she was originally to have been CITY OF RIPON.

In 1970 she became another Ellerman ship to be sold to Ben Line Steamers Ltd., becoming their BENCAIRN. She was eventually broken up at Kaohsiung in 1975.

CITY OF WINCHESTER

William Denny and Bros. Ltd, Dumbarton; 1952, 10594gt.

Ellerman and Bucknall's CITY OF WINCHESTER was identical to CITY OF BRISBANE in almost every way. She too joined Ben Line in 1970, becoming BENVANNOCH, and was also broken up at Kaohsiung in 1975.

CITY OF PORT ELIZABETH
Vickers-Armstrongs Ltd, Newcastle; 1952, 13363gt, 107 passengers.

The only vessels built for the Ellerman group in post-war years with extensive passenger accommodation were a class of four ships for Ellerman and Bucknall's service from London to South and East Africa. In terms of tonnage they were the largest ships the group had yet built, but were surpassed in length by some cargo ships. The choice of Doxford diesels for these ships was notable, especially for a company which had clung to steam machinery for so long.

First of the group was CITY OF PORT ELIZABETH, seen here approaching Tilbury in June 1970. This was her last full year of service, and in 1971 all four of the class were sold to the Greek Karageorgis group, who planned that all would undergo a massive conversion to passenger and vehicle ferries. Although work was started on CITY OF PORT ELIZABETH, and she was renamed first MEDITERRANEAN ISLAND and then MEDITERRANEAN SUN, conversion was never completed, and in 1980 she was towed to Kaohsiung for demolition.

CITY OF EXETER
Vickers-Armstrongs Ltd., Newcastle; 1953, 13345gt, 107 passengers.

CITY OF EXETER was successfully converted to a passenger and car ferry, and as MEDITERRANEAN SEA entered service between Patras and Ancona in late 1972. Having changed the Greek flag for the Cypriot, she is still afloat in 1993.

CITY OF YORK
Vickers-Armstrongs Ltd., Newcastle; 1953, 13345gt, 107 passengers.

The pleasing profile of these ships was marred only by the contemporary trend to have just one full height mast. This forced them to fly their houseflag and any other flags such as courtesy ensigns from the same mast.

CITY OF YORK was converted by Karageorgis, although increasing her passenger capacity to 850 and turning her holds into a garage took the Perama shipyards from 1971 to 1974. She then entered the Ancona to Rhodes service as the Greek flag MEDITERRANEAN SKY, as which she is still afloat.

CITY OF DURBAN
Vickers-Armstrongs Ltd., Newcastle; 1954, 13345gt, 107 passengers.

Seen here in the Thames, CITY OF DURBAN was the last of the class, and had the shortest life. Sold to Karageorgis in 1971, she was renamed MEDITERRANEAN DOLPHIN, but remained laid up at Perama until sold for scrap at Kaohsiung in 1974.

ANATOLIAN
William Gray and Co. Ltd., West Hartlepool; 1955, 3799gt.

By the fifties ships built for the Mediterranean services of Ellerman and Papayanni were little smaller than those intended for the Ellerman group's longer routes. ANATOLIAN had the dubious distinction of being one of the last ships anywhere built with triple expansion engines. Notwithstanding the addition of low pressure turbines, such machinery was obsolescent by 1955.

ANATOLIAN was one of a class of four which spent considerable time transferred or on charter to other companies. Transfers began in 1963 with use on Hall Line's routes, for which she was briefly renamed CITY OF DURHAM. She spent the summers of 1966 and 1968 on charter to the Cunard Steamship Co. Ltd. for their services to the Great Lakes, for which she assumed the name ASCANIA.

After her last Cunard charter she was sold in December 1968, her outmoded machinery condemning her to early redundancy. But she was far from finished, and a variety of owners based in Greece, Cyprus, Pakistan and Sharjah had another ten years' work out of her under the names AGIA SOPHIA, FULKA, KHALID and GULF UNITY. She was broken up at Gadani Beach in 1978.

LANCASTRIAN
William Gray and Co. Ltd., West Hartlepool; 1956, 3799gt.

The career of the steamer LANCASTRIAN ran in parallel with her sister ANATOLIAN. Between 1962 and 1964 LANCASTRIAN worked for Hall Line as CITY OF LEICESTER, and in 1966 she too ran to the Great Lakes as Cunard's ALSATIA. Sold out of the fleet in 1969 she became the Greek-owned, Cyprus-flag THEOKRATES, and then the KHORFAKAN of Sharjah. Under the last name she met a violent end on 12th February 1975. Whilst waiting to unload cement at Sharjah she broke her moorings and was blown ashore, where she was later cut up.

FLAMINIAN
Henry Robb Ltd., Leith; 1956, 3100gt.

Oil engines were finally adopted for the larger Mediterranean traders with the FLORIAN of 1955 and her sister FLAMINIAN, seen here. Built for Westcott and Laurance Lines, she was transferred to Ellerman and Papayanni in 1969. When CITY names were declared obligatory in 1974, she became CITY OF IZMIR, but was sold just a year later. First as CLIMAX PEARL and later as MALDIVE PEARL she finished her years under the flag of the Maldive Islands, being demolished at Gadani Beach in 1984.

ARCADIAN
Henry Robb Ltd., Leith; 1960, 3402gt.

The motorship ARCADIAN was to be the last of the classic cargo liners with engines amidships built for Ellerman and Papayanni. After all ships in the group were registered under the ownership of Ellerman City Liners Ltd she became CITY OF FAMAGUSTA in 1974. In 1977 she was renamed BATROUN under the Lebanese ownership of T. Gargour et fils, and as part of this well-kept fleet of small cargo liners lasted until 1986 when she was broken up at Gadani Beach.

CITY OF COLOMBO CLASS

CITY OF COLOMBO

Barclay, Curle and Co. Ltd., Glasgow; 1956, 7739gt.

After the frenzied ordering by Ellermans in the immediate post-war years, the pace slackened considerably in the fifties. When new building on any scale resumed in 1956 it was with a class of six impressive-looking motorships, beginning with City Line's CITY OF COLOMBO. This photograph of her was taken in October 1971 in a classic location, just off the Albert entrance to Birkenhead Docks.

CITY OF COLOMBO was sold to Ben Line Steamers Ltd. in 1977, and as BENMOHR gave 18 months service before being broken up at Kaohsiung.

BENEDIN

Caledon Shipbuilding and Engineering Co. Ltd., Dundee; 1956, 7716gt.

In 1968 two ships of this class were bareboat chartered by Ben Line Steamers Ltd., CITY OF WINNIPEG becoming BENEDIN. If anything, the class looked even more handsome in the Leith company's simple but dignified livery. Returning to the Ellerman group in 1970, she was renamed CITY OF DELHI under Ellerman and Bucknall management. In 1976 she was sold, and sailed under the Liberian flag for Gulf Shipping Lines Ltd. as FEXL GLORY until broken up at Chittagong in 1980.

CITY OF RIPON
Vickers-Armstrongs (Shipbuilders) Ltd., Newcastle; 1956, 7713gt.

The career of CITY OF RIPON almost exactly paralleled that of CITY OF COLOMBO. She was delivered to City Line a month later, sold to Ben Line Steamers Ltd. in 1970 to become BENVANNOCH, and arrived at Kaohsiung to be scrapped a few months after her sister in 1979.

CITY OF WELLINGTON
Cammell, Laird and Co. (Shipbuilders and Engineers) Ltd., Birkenhead; 1956, 7702gt.

With the Cory collier and a London tug with open wheelhouse, this photograph of CITY OF WELLINGTON is as redolent of the Thames as that above is of the Mersey. Although owned by Hall Line Ltd., as her Liverpool registration suggests, CITY OF WELLINGTON is flying an Ellerman and Bucknall houseflag.

Unlike her colleagues, Ben Line showed no interest in her, but the polyglot Gulf Shipping Lines Ltd. did, and she served under the Singapore flag as EASTERN ENTERPRISE from late 1978 until early 1979 when she was broken up at Kaohsiung.

CITY OF GUILDFORD CLASS

CITY OF GUILDFORD
Swan, Hunter and Wigham Richardson Ltd., Wallsend; 1957, 4945gt.

In 1957 the trend to ever larger cargo liners was reversed with a group of three motorships for Hall Line which had much in common with the moderate-sized Mediterranean traders. The first was CITY OF GUILDFORD, seen here on the Mersey in May 1975.

Despite containerisation, Ellermans had good value out of these ships, all seeing at least twenty years' service. CITY OF GUILDFORD was sold in 1979, becoming in succession the Greek EURYDICE, the Panama-flag MIGHTY SPIRIT and the Maltese NIRAV before ending her days at Chittagong in 1984.

CITY OF LANCASTER
Swan, Hunter and Wigham Richardson Ltd., Wallsend; 1958, 4949gt.

Over 18 months after the CITY OF GUILDFORD, her builders delivered the second of the class, CITY OF LANCASTER, seen here in Dutch waters. Her two sisters had Sulzer diesels built under licence at Sunderland, but those for CITY OF LANCASTER were supplied by Sulzer Brothers themselves. Delivering them from Winterthur in Switzerland to Tyneside must have been an interesting undertaking.

CITY OF LANCASTER came to an ignominious end. On 25th September 1979, not long after she had become the LANCASTER under the Greek flag, she collided with the tanker THISTLE VENTURE in the Irish Sea. She staggered into Dublin and was later towed to her intended destination of Glasgow, where her general cargo and tea from Calcutta were discharged. Here her owners lost interest in her and she was eventually taken over by the Clyde Port Authority. The abandoned ship was sold for scrapping in Spain, where she arrived early in 1982, well over two years after her accident.

CITY OF ST. ALBANS CLASS

CITY OF ST. ALBANS
William Denny and Bros. Ltd., Dumbarton; 1960, 7155gt.

CITY OF ST. ALBANS and her four sisters were virtual repeats of the CITY OF GUILDFORD class, with minor alterations to the superstructure and a radar scanner which boasted its own mast, rather than being perched precariously on the funnel. CITY OF ST. ALBANS was delivered to Ellerman and Bucknall, and is seen here in London docks in June 1976.

She had an eventful career, being shelled by a warship during the Pakistani civil war in 1971, and representing her owners at the Queen's Silver Jubilee Review in the Mersey during June 1977. Sold to Greek owners in 1979 and renamed ISLAND OF MARMARA, she almost immediately collided with the British coaster CONFORMITY. She was broken up at Jamnagar in 1983.

CITY OF LICHFIELD
William Denny and Bros. Ltd., Dumbarton; 1961, 4976gt.

The low April sun catches Ellerman and Bucknall's CITY OF LICHFIELD in 1969, her paintwork at the mercy of unattended Thames lighters.

The end of her career was blighted by a mishap. Sold to Greece in 1978 she was renamed LEEDS and then CITY OF LEEDS, both under the Cypriot flag. On 11th November 1980 she stranded in heavy weather whilst leaving the Turkish port of Antalya. Refloated, abandoned and auctioned, she never traded again, and was broken up at Aliaga in 1984.

CITY OF MELBOURNE
Alexander Stephen and Sons Ltd., Linthouse; 1959, 9914gt.

When built the CITY OF MELBOURNE was one of the most strikingly innovative cargo liners, not just of the Ellerman fleet but of the entire British merchant navy. Although helping to accelerate the trend to engines three quarters aft, this large Sulzer-engined reefer still had the split superstructure which had been a feature of cargo ships since the turn of the century.

She was built for Ellerman and Bucknall's Australian trade, and is shown at Swansea in August 1963. With the advent of refrigerated container ships, she was switched to the company's South African routes, being renamed CITY OF CAPETOWN. After her Ellerman career she spent a year under the Singapore flag as OTAGOLD before being sold to Kaohsiung breakers in 1979.

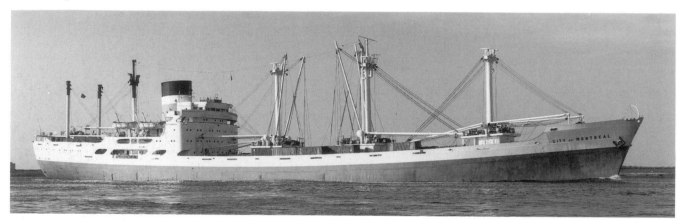

CITY OF MONTREAL
Barclay, Curle and Co. Ltd., Glasgow; 1960, 10551gt.

CITY OF SYDNEY was a development of Ellerman and Bucknall's CITY OF MELBOURNE with the fourth hatch moved from the bridge deck to give a more solid-looking, built up superstructure. Containerisation of the Australian trade saw her move to Canadian services, for which she was renamed CITY OF MONTREAL in 1971, as seen here.

After a comparatively short career of 17 years with the group, she was sold to Hong Kong owners who put her under the Panama flag as YAT FEI. But diesels that could propel her at seventeen knots probably made her uneconomic as a tramp, and in 1979 she was demolished at Kaohsiung.

CITY OF CANBERRA *see opposite*

Fig. 4.—Engine-room of the " Freshwater."

at a pressure of 350 ℔ per sq. in. As a stand-by, there is a Hamworthy compressor with a capacity of 6 cu. ft. per minute at a pressure of 350 ℔ per sq. in., and this unit is

driven by a Lister-Blackstone 5-H.P. Diesel engine. Separate lines from the receivers supply air to the generators, whistle and sea-inlet weed-cleaning system. Lubrication of the main engine is carried out by engine-driven pumps, with one Hamworthy motor-driven pump provided for emergency duties. Included in the system are Serck coolers and Zwicky filters. Lubricating oils and greases for the main and auxiliary machinery have been supplied by Shell-Mex and B.P., Ltd., of London.

A De Laval fuel-oil purifier, which is fitted with twin pumps, is installed, and a Heatrae four-element heater deals with fuel-oil heating.

Ventilation of the engine-room is by two aerofoil fans, supplied by Messrs. Woods of Colchester, Ltd.

Direct current at a tension of 225 volts for lighting, power and the electrically-driven auxiliaries is provided by two Mawdsley's 60-kW. generators, each of which is driven by a Crossley type-B.W.G./11 Diesel engine running at 1,100 r.p.m.

The electrical installation has been carried out by Messrs. Telford, Grier, Mackay & Co., Ltd., of Glasgow, who have also supplied the switchboards, which incorporate Whipp and Bourne circuit-breakers.

An Exide 12-volt battery is installed for emergency lighting duties.

Sanitary water is supplied by a Mono type-M60 motor-driven pump. A similar pump is installed for the domestic fresh-water supply to the gravity tank on the bridge deck.

Also installed are a Turbulo oily-water separator and a Mono oily bilge-water pump. K.D.G. hydrostatic contents gauges are fitted in connection with the fuel-oil tanks, while a hand-operated emergency fire and bilge pump has been provided by Messrs. James Young & Cunningham, Ltd., of Glasgow.

The Shipbuilding Conference

AT the annual general meeting of the Shipbuilding Conference, held in London on the 15th October, Colonel T. Eustace Smith, C.B.E., T.D., D.L., J.P., was elected as President. He succeeds Sir James Milne, C.B.E., who is chairman and managing director of Messrs. J. Samuel White and Co., Ltd., of Cowes, Isle of Wight. Mr. Alexander H. White, C.B.E., who is deputy chairman of Messrs. Lithgows, Ltd., of Port Glasgow, was elected Vice-President of the Conference.

Colonel Eustace Smith is chairman and managing director of Smith's Dock Co., Ltd., of South Bank-on-Tees and North Shields, and is of the fifth generation of his family to be in control of the company. Educated at Eton, he served an apprenticeship with Messrs. R. & W. Hawthorn, Leslie and Co., Ltd., and with Smith's Dock Co., Ltd., and later studied engineering at Leeds University. Colonel Smith joined the company in 1923 and became sole managing director in 1952; in 1956, he was elected chairman.

Colonel T. Eustace Smith, C.B.E., T.D., D.L., J.P.

Mr. Alexander H. White, C.B.E., began his career with the Fairfield Shipbuilding and Engineering Co., Ltd., Govan, Glasgow, where he eventually controlled the estimating and buying departments. In 1940, he went to the Admiralty as personal assistant to the late Sir James Lithgow, an appointment which was followed by those of Regional Officer for Scotland of the Merchant Shipbuilding Division of the Admiralty and of Assistant Director of the Department in Charge of Materials and Priorities. At the end of the war, Mr. White joined Messrs. Lithgows, Ltd., as secretary and became, in turn, a director in 1948, managing director in 1950

and deputy chairman in 1952. He is also a director of a number of companies within the Lithgow Group, notably the Fairfield Shipbuilding and Engineering Co., Ltd., Messrs. William Hamilton & Co., Ltd., Port Glasgow, and Rankin and Blackmore Ltd., Greenock. Mr. White was made a Commander of the Order of the British Empire in the Birthday Honours List this year.

Mr. Alexander H. White, C.B.E.

"CITY OF MELBOURNE"

Ellerman Ship with the most Powerful British-built Diesel Engine

SPECIALLY designed for the carriage of general and refrigerated cargoes between the United Kingdom, Canada and Australia, the single-screw motorship *City of Melbourne* has recently been delivered to the Ellerman Lines, Ltd., of London, by Messrs. Alexander Stephen and Sons, Ltd., of Linthouse, Glasgow.

Externally, the vessel presents a graceful picture with a raked stem, neat cruiser stern and three masts. The attractive superstructure is arranged aft of amidships to suit the position of the machinery.

Constructed as a complete superstructure vessel and in accordance with the requirements of Lloyd's Register of Shipping, for the classification ✠ 100 A.1 with refrigeration, the *City of Melbourne* is powered by a Stephen-Sulzer, type-12RSAD76, 12-cylinder, supercharged Diesel engine, moderately rated to develop 14,000 B.H.P. at 114·5 r.p.m. This is the most powerful Diesel engine yet to be constructed in Britain and on test developed 18,220 B.H.P. at 126 r.p.m. The principal dimensions and other leading characteristics appear in Table I.

Subdivision of the hull, as shown on Plate XVII., provides five main cargo holds, with corresponding lower and upper 'tween-deck spaces. No. 2 lower and No. 3 upper and lower 'tween decks, together with No. 4 hold, are insulated for the carriage of frozen or fruit cargoes. Chilled cargoes may also be carried in No. 2 lower and No. 3 upper 'tween-deck spaces.

Deep tanks interposed between Nos. 2 and 3 holds are suitable for the carriage of latex, mineral oil, vegetable oil or general cargo, and are coated with vinyl lacquer. For filling and discharging cargo oil, there is a Drysdale Vertoil rotary electric pump, of 100 tons per hour, which is located in a separate pump room.

For the carriage of grain in bulk, No. 1 hold and No. 5 hold and lower 'tween decks, as well as the deep cargo and ballast tanks, can be suitably fitted out.

As shown in Table II., the vessel has storage capacity for nearly 2,500 tons of fuel oil and more than 4,400 tons of water ballast, while her grain cubic for uninsulated cargo, as given in Table III., is in excess of 616,000 cu. ft., measured to top of beam and inside of shell.

TABLE I.—PRINCIPAL DIMENSIONS AND OTHER LEADING PARTICULARS OF THE "CITY OF MELBOURNE"

Length overall	545ft. 1⅝in.
Length B.P.	510ft. 0in.
Breadth moulded	71ft. 0in.
Breadth extreme	71ft. 4in.
Depth moulded to shelter deck	43ft. 6in.
Depth moulded to second deck	33ft. 6in.
Lightweight, tons	7,900
Lightship V.C.G.	30·4ft.
Lightship L.C.G. aft of amidships	33·9ft.
Load draught	28ft. 9¼in.
Corresponding deadweight, tons	12,300
Corresponding displacement, tons	20,200
Block coefficient at load draught	0·676
T.P.I. at load draught	68·25
Service B.H.P.	14,000
Corresponding r.p.m.	114·5

TABLE II.—TANK CAPACITIES

Compartment.	Frames.	Fuel Oil at 40 cu. ft./ton.	Diesel Oil at 41·2 cu. ft./ton.	Fresh-water at 36 cu. ft./ton.	Feed Water at 36 cu. ft./ton.	Water Ballast.	Cargo Oil, cu. ft.
Double-bottom tanks.—							
No. 1	162-185	—	—	222·0	—	227·7	—
No. 2, P.	127-162	—	—	—	—	213·4	—
No. 2, S.	127-162	—	—	—	—	214·3	—
No. 3, P.	89-127	219·7	—	—	—	251·0	—
No. 3, Cr.	89-127	173·7	—	—	—	198·5	—
No. 3, S.	89-125	219·7	—	—	—	251·0	—
No. 4, P.	69- 89	112·1	—	—	—	128·1	—
No. 4, Cr.	69- 89	99·0	—	—	—	113·2	—
No. 4, S.	69- 89	112·1	—	—	—	128·1	—
No. 5 (Diesel oil o/flow), P.	66- 69	—	23·4	—	—	—	—
No. 5 (fuel oil o/flow), S.	66- 69	24·1	—	—	—	—	—
No. 6, P.	51- 66	—	116·5	—	—	—	—
No. 6, S.	51- 66	—	116·5	—	—	—	—
No. 7, P.	40- 50	—	—	—	53·3	—	—
No. 7, S.	40- 50	—	—	—	53·4	—	—
No. 8 (deep), P.	29- 39	114·6	—	—	—	165·3	—
No. 8 (deep), S.	29- 39	126·2	—	—	—	144·2	—
No. 9 (deep)	21- 28	—	—	81·6	—	83·7	—
Total, double-bottom tanks		1,231·2	256·4	303·6	106·7	2,118·5	—
Fore-peak tank	185-Stem	—	—	112·0	—	114·8	—
Aft-peak tank	0- 10	—	—	101·9	—	104·5	—
Total, double-bottom and peak tanks		1,231·2	256·4	517·5	106·7	2,337·8	—
Fuel-oil cross-bunker, P.	30- 99	213·3	—	—	—	244·4	—
Fuel-oil cross-bunker, Cr.	90- 99	200·0	—	—	—	228·6	—
Fuel-oil cross-bunker, S.	90- 99	213·9	—	—	—	244·4	—
Forward fuel-oil side bunker, P.	59- 69	130·0	—	—	—	—	—
Forward fuel-oil side bunker, S.	59- 69	130·0	—	—	—	—	—
After fuel-oil side bunker, P.	51- 59	113·2	—	—	—	—	—
After fuel-oil side bunker, S.	51 59	113·2	—	—	—	—	—
Fuel-oil settling tank, P.	62- 67	26·0	—	—	—	—	—
Fuel-oil settling tank, S.	62- 67	26·0	—	—	—	—	—
Fuel-oil ready-use tank, P.	57- 62	26·2	—	—	—	—	—
Fuel-oil ready-use tank, S.	57- 62	26·2	—	—	—	—	—
Diesel-oil settling tank, P.	67- 69	—	10·0	—	—	—	—
Diesel-oil ready-use tank, inboard, S.	67- 69	—	5·0	—	—	—	—
Diesel-oil ready-use tank, outboard, S.	67- 69	—	5·0	—	—	—	—
Total bunkers, etc.		1,218·6	20·0	—	—	717·4	—
No. 2 hold lower deep tank, P.	127-135	—	—	—	—	317·7	11,120
No. 2 hold lower deep tank, S.	127-135	—	—	—	—	317·7	11,120
No. 2 hold upper deep tank, P.	128-134	—	—	—	—	228·4	7,995
No. 2 hold upper deep tank, S.	128-134	—	—	—	—	228·4	7,995
No. 2 hold ballast tank, P.	127-134	—	—	—	—	146·0	—
No. 2 hold ballast tank, S.	127-134	—	—	—	—	145·9	—
Total deep and ballast tanks		—	—	—	—	1,384·1	38,230
Grand totals		2,449·8	276·4	517·5	106·7	4,439·3	38,230

As already mentioned, the *City of Melbourne* has been built as a complete superstructure vessel and the scantlings of the main structural members are shown in the midship section reproduced in Fig. 2. While the ship was in the river during the fitting-out period, the submerged surfaces of the hull were protected against corrosion by the Guardion cathodic protection system.

Prior to handing over, the vessel was inclined to ascertain her stability ; and from the results of this experiment, the lightship worked out as 7,900 tons, with a vertical centre of gravity 30·4ft. above the base and an L.C.G. 33·9ft. abaft amidships. This lightweight is made up as follows :—

	Tons
Net steel	4,470
Wood and outfit	1,920
Machinery	1,510
Lightweight	7,900

With the freeboard working out at 4ft. 10¼in., the load draught to the bottom of keel is 28ft. 9¼in., which gives a displacement of 20,200 tons and a deadweight of 12,300 tons. At this draught, the block coefficient (CB) is 0·676 and the tons per in. immersion (TPI) 68·25. From these basic figures, a comprehensive range of voyage conditions were calculated and details of these are given in Tables IV. and V.

ACCOMMODATION

A suite of rooms for the captain, comprising a dayroom, bedroom and bathroom, is arranged on the captain's bridge. Veneers in French walnut with sycamore trim are used for the walls of the dayroom, while the bedroom is painted.

Large cabins on the boat deck are provided for the remainder of the ship's officers. Accommodated in the after house are the chief engineer and the other engine-room officers ; while the chief, second and radio officers' cabins, together with the ship's offices, are arranged in the forward house. There is a comfortable smoking room, panelled in fiddle-back sycamore with trim of African mahogany.

TABLE III.—CAPACITIES OF CARGO SPACES

Compartment.	Frames.	Uninsulated. Cubic Feet.			Insulated. Cubic Feet.	
		Grain.	Cotton.	Bale.	Gross.	Net.
		Top of Beam Inside Shell.	Top of Beam Inside Sparring.	Bottom of Beam Inside Sparring.	Underside of Roof Insulation or Meat Rails to Deck and Face of Permanent Battens.	Underside of Roof Insulation or Meat Rails to Gratings or Dunnage and Face of Permanent Battens.
No. 1 hold	162-185	24,250	22,520	20,705	—	—
No. 2 hold	135-162	77,835	73,300	69,100	—	—
No. 2 hold, lower deep tank, P.	127-135	11,140	10,400	9,820	—	—
No. 2 hold, lower deep tank, S.	127-135	11,140	10,400	9,820	—	—
No. 3 hold	99-127	93,830	89,890	84,320	—	—
No. 4 hold	70- 89	—	—	—	57,080	55,605
No. 5 hold	10- 39	35,710	33,785	31,205	—	—
Total holds and lower deep tanks....		253,905	240,295	224,970	57,080	55,605
No. 1 lower 'tween decks	162-155	22,925	21,610	20,155	—	—
No. 2 lower 'tween decks, Cr.	134-152	17,340	17,130	16,585	—	—
No. 2 lower 'tween decks, S.	134-162	—	—	—	11,490	11,270
No. 2 lower 'tween decks, P.	134-162	—	—	—	11,670	11,445
No. 2 hold, upper deep tank, P.	128-134	8,010	7,640	7,160	—	—
No. 2 hold, upper deep tank, S.	128-134	8,010	7,640	7,160	—	—
No. 3 lower 'tween decks, Cr., forward	101-119	17,370	17,370	16,825	—	—
No. 3 lower 'tween decks, S.	89-127	—	—	—	20,875	20,460
No. 3 lower 'tween decks, Cr., aft	89-101	—	—	—	7,970	7,810
No. 3 lower 'tween decks, P.	89-127	—	—	—	21,330	20,910
No. 4 lower 'tween decks	70- 89	32,715	31,995	29,070	—	—
No. 5 lower 'tween decks	7- 39	42,130	40,730	37,025	—	—
Total lower 'tween decks and upper deep tanks		148,500	144,115	133,980	73,335	71,895
No. 1 upper 'tween decks	162-185	25,845	24,830	23,710	—	—
No. 2 upper 'tween decks	134-162	48,485	47,370	45,005	—	—
No. 2 hold, ballast tank, P.	127-134	5,110	4,960	4,700	—	—
No. 2 hold, ballast tank, S.	127-134	5,105	4,955	4,695	—	—
No. 3 upper 'tween decks, Cr.	101-119	16,610	16,610	16,345	—	—
No. 3 upper 'tween decks, forward, S.	107-127	—	—	—	9,255	9,010
No. 3 upper 'tween decks, forward, P.	107-127	—	—	—	9,560	9,305
No. 3 upper 'tween decks, aft, S.	89-107	—	—	—	9,440	9,185
No. 3 upper 'tween decks, aft, P.	89-107	—	—	—	9,515	9,260
No. 4 upper 'tween decks, excl. hatchway and trunk	68- 89	37,390	36,660	35,945	—	—
No. 4 hatchway and trunk	72- 84	8,695	8,605	8,605	—	—
Bonded cargo locker, P.	60- 68	5,105	4,935	4,665	—	—
Tonnage well	38- 40	3,785	3,715	3,580	—	—
No. 5 upper 'tween decks, excl. hatchway and trunk	10- 38	45,520	44,565	42,555	—	—
No. 5 hatchway and trunk	15- 31	11,595	11,470	11,470	—	—
Total upper 'tween decks, ballast tanks, hatchways and trunks		213,245	208,675	201,275	37,770	36,760
Hazardous cargo store (shelter deck)	155½-158½	585	505	445	—	—
Grand totals		616,235	593,590	560,670	168,185	164,260

Cabins in the midship houses on the shelter deck are provided for the purser, junior ship and engineer officers, cadets and petty officers. There is also a hospital and surgery for the European crew. Arranged in close proximity to the large pantry and well-equipped galley is the dining saloon, which is panelled in Australian silver ash, with the window surrounds in toned sycamore and the glazed entrance door in Queensland walnut.

Adjacent to the dining saloon is a small duty mess, panelled in Warerite Tersuto azure blue.

Comfortable four-berth rooms are arranged on the shelter and second decks for the Asian crew and on the poop deck there are two Asian galleys.

Special attention has been given to the ventilation and heating of the European and Asian accommodation, the plant having been provided by Winsor Engineering Marine, Ltd., of Hillington, Glasgow. Pleno-units give a heated mechanical supply to the cabins, which are naturally exhausted. Cold mechanical supply and mechanical exhaust are arranged for the galleys. Air-conditioning is provided in the dining saloon, duty mess, smoking room and European hospital.

EQUIPMENT

For cargo handling there are six 5-ton, four 7-ton, eight 10-ton and one 20-ton derricks, all but two of which are served by Clarke-Chapman electrically-operated winches of

TABLE IV.—VOYAGE CONDITIONS

Ref.	Voyage.	Fuel Oil.	Diesel Oil.	Fresh-water.	Stores.	Crew and Effects.	Cargo.	Water Ballast.	Dead-weight.	Light-weight.	Displacement.
1	Lightship	—	—	—	—	—	—	—	—	7,900	7,900
2	Departure from St. Lawrence	746	59	522	114	15	7,012	428	8,896	7,900	16,796
3	Arrival Curaçao	445	40	408	105	15	7,012	428	8,453	7,900	16,353
4	Departure from Curaçao	2,425	253	522	124	15	7,012	428	10,779	7,900	18,679
5	Arrival at Brisbane.............	1,521	195	181	98	15	7,012	428	9,450	7,900	17,350
6	Departure from Brisbane	1,512	184	219	120	15	6,219	428	8,697	7,900	16,597
7	Arrival at Melbourne	1,404	176	170	117	15	6,219	428	8,529	7,900	16,429
8	Departure from Melbourne	1,215	92	624	118	15	7,055	428	9,547	7,900	17,447
8L	Departure from Melbourne with lead	1,215	92	624	118	15	9,377	—	11,441	7,900	19,341
9	Arrival at Aden	445	40	380	99	15	7,055	428	8,462	7,900	16,362
9L	Arrival at Aden with lead	445	40	380	99	15	9,377	—	10,356	7,900	18,256
10	Departure from Aden	1,745	193	364	118	15	7,055	428	9,918	7,900	17,818
10L	Departure from Aden with lead ..	1,745	193	364	118	15	9,377	—	11,812	7,900	19,712
11	Arrival at Rotterdam	1,174	154	185	104	15	7,055	428	9,115	7,900	17,015
11L	Arrival at Rotterdam with lead....	1,174	154	185	104	15	9,377	—	11,009	7,900	18,909
12	Departure from Rotterdam	1,157	127	376	91	15	1,140	2,513	5,419	7,900	13,319
13	Arrival at Liverpool	Very similar to 12. Oil, water, etc., consumed about 120 tons.									
12L	Departure from Rotterdam with lead	1,157	127	376	91	15	2,140	2,513	6,419	7,900	14,319
13L	Arrival at Liverpool with lead	Very similar to 12L. Oil, water, etc., consumed about 120 tons.									
14	Departure from Liverpool	1,074	110	624	118	15	—	3,192	5,133	7,900	13,033
15	Arrival St. Lawrence coasting in ballast	773	91	505	109	15	—	3,192	4,685	7,900	12,585
16	Arrival Port Pirie coasting with lead	1,307	145	375	117	15	—	1,812	3,771	7,900	11,671
16L	Departure Port Pirie coasting with grain	1,303	140	362	116	15	2,500	—	4,436	7,900	12,336
17	Departure from Geelong coasting with grain and lead............	1,303	140	394	116	15	3,425	797	6,190	7,900	14,090
17L	Departure from Geelong	1,240	135	390	116	15	5,675	369	7,940	7,900	15,840
18	Docking	200	20	384	80	15	—	1,520	2,219	7,900	10,119
19	Homogeneous departure. Cargo 81·9 cu. ft./ton	2,425	253	624	130	15	8,853	—	12,300	7,900	20,200
20	Homogeneous arrival	200	20	100	80	15	8,853	428	9,696	7,900	17,596

the Autocon pattern. The remaining two are served by contactor-type winches, which, in addition to cargo handling, are used for warping.

MacGregor patent sliding steel hatch covers are fitted to the weather-deck hatchways, and special MacGregor flush hinging covers are installed for the hatchways serving No. 4 insulated hold. Roller beams are fitted to the 'tween-deck hatchways.

Steering is by means of a Hastie four-ram electro-hydraulic steering gear, which is controlled by telemotor from the wheelhouse and mechanically from the poop deck.

For life-saving purposes there are four Watercraft glass-fibre lifeboats, one of which is motor-propelled, and these craft are carried in Bi-Luff davits.

All the cargo spaces, as well as the engine-room, are protected against fire by the Kidde-Rich CO_2 combined detecting and extinguishing system. Of the automatic type, the system incorporates two visual smoke-detecting cabinets, one situated adjacent to the CO_2-cylinder room and the other in the wheelhouse.

The refrigerating plant to deal with the cooling of No. 2 lower 'tween decks, No. 3 lower and upper 'tween decks and No. 4 hold—ten compartments in all—has been supplied by Messrs. J. & E. Hall, Ltd., of Dartford. All the refrigerated spaces are suitable for the carriage of frozen cargoes or fruit. No. 3 upper 'tween decks is also fitted out for the carriage of chilled beef and No. 2 lower 'tween decks for further chilled beef.

Together with the brine room and the refrigeration spare-gear store, the refrigerating plant is situated on the second deck to starboard, abreast the main-engine casing. The plant consists of three Veebloc eight-cylinder compressors (using Arcton refrigerant) directly coupled to 97-B.H.P. electric motors, three condensers and three evaporators, all of the shell and tube type.

Air is circulated by Axia reversible fans of the axial-flow pattern, and there is a system of Elliott electrical distant-reading thermometers working on the three wire " null "-point system. Nine portable ozone-generating sets are also installed.

To eliminate sweating at the boundaries of the insulated spaces, there is a Thermotank system of thermal injection. Electric cables are applied as closely as possible to the cold metallic surface to concentrate the injected heat on to the steel. The electric cables consist of a conductor core, magnesium oxide insulation and a copper sheath. Cables 0·228-in in diameter are used and they are protected by a stout metal cover which is thermally insulated.

Rocksil, held in position by resin-bonded plywood, supplied and fitted by the Cork Insulation & Asbestos Co., Ltd., of London, is used to insulate the cold chambers. An interesting feature is that the insulated cargo doors, cooler access doors and provision-chamber doors are of reinforced polyester resin with polyurethene foam filling in lieu of the normal teak and Rocksil and that the insulating medium for the MacGregor hatch covers to No. 4 insulated hold is also polyurethene foam.

Aids to navigation include a Sperry gyro-compass ; magnetic compass ; Marconi Seagraph III. echo sounding gear, Lodestone direction-finder, wireless and radar ; Decca Navigator ; and Robinson electric engine and steering telegraphs. A Commodore log of the side streaming type is also fitted.

In general, awnings have been omitted, the insulation over the accommodation having been increased to compensate. There is, however, an aluminium sun awning fitted over the poop deckhouse.

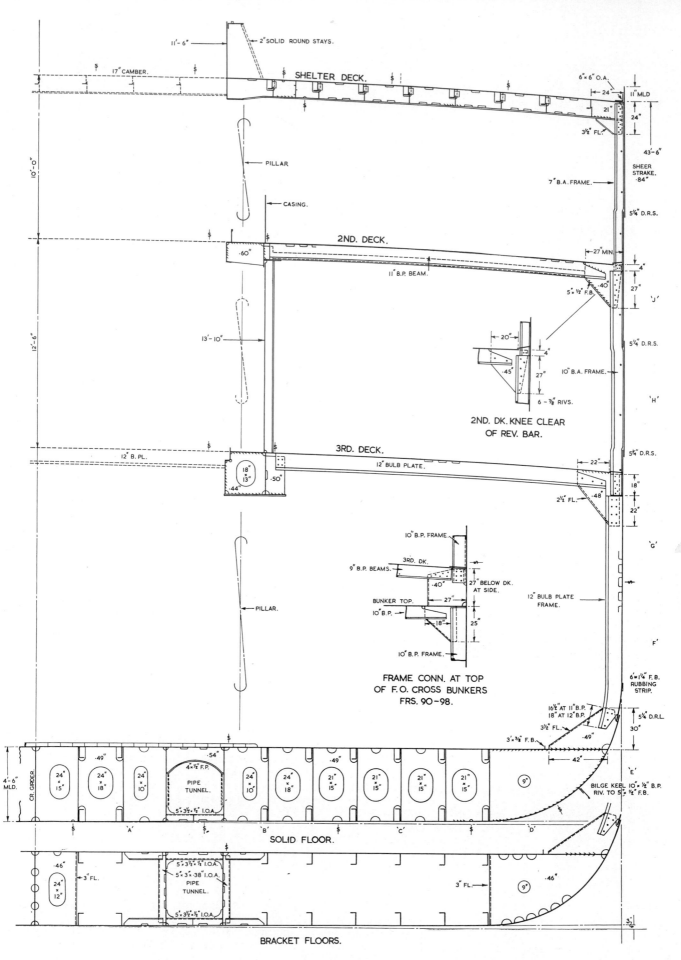

Fig. 2.—Structural Sections.

2

KOTA CANTIK
Vickers Armstrongs (Shipbuilders) Ltd., Newcastle; 1962; 7340gt

This aerial view shows how the three-quarters aft design developed, with four masts and five holds ahead of the bridge. Ellerman and Bucknall's CITY OF EASTBOURNE was renamed CITY OF TORONTO for Canadian services in 1971. Redundant in 1978 she became KOTA CANTIK of Singapore's Pacific International Lines (Pte.) Ltd. as seen here. She was broken up at Kaohsiung in 1984.

CITY OF OTTAWA
Vickers-Armstrongs (Shipbuilders) Ltd., Newcastle; 1963, 7342gt.

This view of the CITY OF OTTAWA in Birkenhead's West Float in March 1976 is full of interest, showing Ellerman liners at berths which the company had made its own. Astern is CITY OF LANCASTER, making full use of her own cargo gear despite the apparently adequate provision of quayside cranes.

A sister of CITY OF EASTBOURNE, she began life as Ellerman and Bucknall's CITY OF GLASGOW, and was renamed CITY OF OTTAWA in 1971: the maple leaf on her funnel in this shot being a relic of her Canadian service.

In 1978 she was sold to the Singapore-based owners who had bought her sister, and ran as KOTA CAHAYA. Mainland Chinese breakers bought her in 1985.

CITY OF CANBERRA *(opposite)*
Barclay, Curle and Co. Ltd., Glasgow; 1961, 10543gt.

The three-quarters aft design in the Ellerman and Bucknall fleet was further refined in the CITY OF CANBERRA, the major external differences from the CITY OF MONTREAL being the relocation of a topmast from the second to the third mast, and the replacement of the mast on the bridge deck by a pair of kingposts. In 1977 she was sold to Singapore owners whose choice of the name TASGOLD reflected her continued involvement in the reefer trade from Australia. Her end came in a Kaohsiung scrapyard in 1980 before she had reached her nineteenth birthday.

LATER MEDITERRANEAN TRADERS

CORTIAN
A/B Lodose Varv., Lodose; 1962, 537gt.

The size of the waves in the Mersey emphasises that CORTIAN was one of the smallest Ellerman and Papayanni ships. Prior to 1966 she was owned in Sweden as CORTIA, and reverted to this name when Ellerman disposed of her in 1971. In 1974 this little motor coaster was sold to Italy and rechristened AUSTERITY. She was converted into a livestock carrier in 1978, as which she has run with the names BRUNO ALPINA and SIBA FOGGIA.

CITY OF ATHENS
Henry Robb Ltd., Leith; 1967, 1523gt.

In 1974, the remaining Ellerman's Wilson Line cargo ships were given City names, having been registered under the ownership of Ellerman City Liners the previous year. CITY OF ATHENS had been SALMO, one of five "S" class ships built at Leith. All were sold when replaced by full container ships in 1978, CITY OF ATHENS becoming the Panamanian ALDEBARAN II and later the Cypriot ARGIRO. As the Pakistani-owned AL AMEEN she was broken up at Gadani Beach in 1988.

CITY OF ISTANBUL
Henry Robb Ltd., Leith; 1968, 1460gt.

Seen here in the Thames in July 1975, CITY OF ISTANBUL had carried the name MEDITERRANIAN until the previous year. She was the last vessel built for Ellerman and Papayanni, and although following the company's style the curious spelling of her name did give rise to a number of wry comments. Unusually, she found a British buyer when Ellermans sold her after just ten years, and until 1983 she ran as the FENCHURCH of Gracechurch Shipping Ltd. of Newcastle. Greek owners then bought her and renamed her PELOR.

CITY OF MILAN
A. Vuijk en Zonen, Capelle a/d Ijsel; 1969, 930gt.

When full containerisation came to Ellerman's Iberian Peninsula and Mediterranean services in 1970, eight "Hustler" class containerships were chartered from Sea Containers Ltd. At first they were given names of rivers, a few of which - including MINHO - had been used by Leyland Line ships. In 1974, City names were adopted, and MINHO became CITY OF MILAN, as pictured here in March 1977.

Delivery of new and faster ships in 1978 and 1979 saw the ships returned to their owners, and CITY OF MILAN was sold to become the Panama-flag ECO MONDEGO.

CITY OF PERTH
Appledore Shipbuilders Ltd., Appledore; 1979, 1599gt.

The chartered "Hustler" class was replaced by a group of purpose-built containerships which were leased by Ellerman City Liners from a variety of financial organisations. In 1985 CITY OF PERTH was given a new name to better reflect her service, CITY OF LISBON. She was sold to a Hamburg owner in 1988, and became the Cypriot flag ERKA SUN.

URBINO
Earle's Shipbuilding and Engineering Co. Ltd., Hull; 1918, 5199gt.

Although Wilson Line maintained much of its autonomy under Ellerman ownership, over the years occasional ships were transferred to the parent company. URBINO, for instance, emerged from lay-up in 1933 to change her colours but not her name to run under Ellerman and Bucknall management. However, the observant will note that in this photograph she is flying Hall Lines' flag. URBINO was originally intended to be the war standard ship WAR SEAL, but had been bought on the stocks by Ellerman's Wilson Line.

Much of her war years were spent in relative safety on feeder services along the African coast. Despite being extensively overhauled by her builders in post-war years her machinery was clearly worn out and recurrent engine failures led to her being broken up at Faslane in 1954.

CITY OF RIPON
Russell and Co., Port Glasgow; 1915, 6394gt

CITY OF RIPON was built as LEPANTO for the Wilson's trans-Atlantic service just before the takeover by Ellerman. She was transferred to Hall Line ownership and renamed in 1934, and in this photograph her funnel but not her hull has been repainted.

On 11th November 1942 whilst bound from Port Said to New York in ballast she was torpedoed by U-160 off Trinidad and sank with heavy loss of life, there being only 27 survivors from the 83 on board.

SACRAMENTO (top), CITY OF BRISTOL (centre) and 30 DE NOVIEMBRE (bottom)
Cammell Laird and Co. Ltd., Birkenhead; 1945, 7096gt.

After a respectably long career with Ellerman's Wilson Line, the twin screw motor vessel SACRAMENTO was transferred to Ellerman and Bucknall ownership in 1964, serving for four years as CITY OF BRISTOL. Sold in 1969, she spent a year as the FELICIE, and then joined the state-owned Cuban fleet as 30 DE NOVIEMBRE. The final photograph shows her as this, anchored in the Clyde in July 1977 awaiting a berth at Faslane where she was to be demolished.

RAPALLO
Henry Robb Ltd., Leith; 1960, 3402gt.

This is a relatively rare photograph of an Ellerman ship in the Ribble, taken in April 1973 soon after RAPALLO had been transferred to the ownership of Ellerman City Liners and painted up the Ellerman funnel. In 1975 she was further standardised by becoming CITY OF LIMASSOL. This motor vessel spent her last nine years under the Lebanese flag, running as BEITEDDINE until being scrapped in Spain in 1986.

THE LAST CARGO LINERS

CITY OF YORK
Bremer Vulkan A.G., Vegesack; 1976, 7691gt.

By 1976 the Ellerman group had largely given up both designing its own ships and owning them. CITY OF YORK was the second of three "Bremen Progress" standard ships; Ellerman's previous ships from her builders had been First World War reparations tonnage. She was owned by Lloyds Leasing Ltd. and leased to Ellerman City Liners.

Two of her sister ships were sold after just five years' service, but CITY OF YORK survived until 1986 when she became in turn the Cypriot-flag VICMAN, and the JOY and EMERALD under the Greek flag.

CHARTERED SHIPS

CITY OF ATHENS
Sir J. Laing and Sons Ltd., Sunderland; 1945, 8965gt.

Prior to the sixties Ellermans chartered few vessels, but one of the exceptions was herself a remarkable ship. She had been laid down during the war as a "Standard Fast" tanker, part of a group which mostly became Royal Fleet Auxiliaries of the "Wave" class, and was completed for John I. Jacobs and Co. Ltd. as BEECHWOOD. In 1955 she was converted to dry cargo and sold to Italian owners, who placed her under the Panama flag and chartered her to Ellermans as CITY OF ATHENS. Completing her charter in 1957 she was renamed MARIANNE, but her modifications had not come to an end and in 1962 she had her steam turbines replaced with an oil engine. As the Panama-flag but Hong Kong-owned CONSTELLATION and later GOLDEN MOON she ran for another decade, being broken up in Kaohsiung in 1973.

ESTREMADURIAN
Traveweft G.m.b.H., Lubeck; 1958, 1921gt.

A rash of chartering brought a variety of ships to Ellerman and Papayanni services in the late sixties and early seventies. Hired in 1968, the motor vessel ESTREMADURIAN was one of the largest, having been built as VARODD for Norwegian owners, to which name she reverted when her two-year charter was completed. In 1975 John S. Latsis bought her and, despite her being a dry cargo ship, renamed her PETROLA XL and later PETROLA 40 under the Greek flag.

SEA LADY
Robb Caledon Shipbuilders Ltd., Dundee; 1971, 7053gt

Entering Liverpool early one August morning in 1988, the last cargo liner built to an Ellerman design has been reduced to tramping. Since her sale after only nine years' service, CITY OF HULL had already carried the names ST. JOHN and SEAGULL. As the Greek SEA LADY, seen here, she is still listed in Lloyds Register for 1993.

INDEX OF SHIPS
Names in capitals are those carried by ships in photographs.